Contents

Geranium ×*oxonianum*
'Bregover Pearl'

Gardening with Hardy Geraniums

BIRGITTE HUSTED BENDTSEN

Timber Press
Portland · Cambridge

For Lars, Kamilla and Lasse

As with any fairy tale, there were dangers and
obstacles to overcome before the story reached its
happy ending.

Fortunately, the fates ordained that four garden
enthusiasts should cross paths, making this book
project possible. The fairy tale lives on!

Thanks to
Kirsten, May-Britt and Vita.

English language edition copyright © 2005 by Birgitte Husted Bendtsen
and Forlaget Geranium. All rights reserved.

First published with the title *Storkenaeb—bogen om Geranium* by Forlaget
Geranium, Denmark 2003.
Copyright © 2003 Birgitte Husted Bendtsen and Forlaget Geranium.

Photographs by Birgitte Husted Bendtsen, unless otherwise stated.
Graphic design by Kirsten Lyng.
Printed in China.

Published in 2005 by
Timber Press, Inc.

The Haseltine Building
133 S.W. Second Avenue, Suite 450
Portland, Oregon 97204-3527, U.S.A.
www.timberpress.com

Timber Press
2 Station Road
Swavesey
Cambridge CB4 5QJ, U.K.

Library of Congress Cataloging-in-Publication Data
Bendtsen, Birgitte Husted.
  [Storkenæb. English]
  Gardening with hardy geraniums / Birgitte Husted Bendtsen.
     p. cm.
  Includes bibliographical references and index.
  ISBN 0-88192-716-3 (hardback)
  1. Hardy geraniums. I. Title.
  SB413.G35B4313 2005
  635.9'379–dc22

                                        2005002029

A catalogue record for this book is also available from the British Library.

Foreword

Hardy geraniums are among the most popular of hardy perennials. They're adaptable and they're easy to grow but at the same time they require just enough attention during the season and just enough thoughtful care in their placing in the garden to make us think—though not to think so hard that we're discouraged.

They also now come in a vast variety of forms: from neat mounds to vigorous ground covers and there are even a few which climb into neighbouring shrubs. They also come in so many variants on the familiar and artfully simple flower shape, and in so many nuances of colour in what no longer seems to be a narrow range of shades. Even the foliage, once considered mainly as simply the background to the flowers, now demands attention in its own right.

All these developments have inspired enormous enthusiasm among an ever-increasing number of devotees. But it's an exceptional enthusiast who transforms that devotion into a book. One such champion of the hardy geranium is the Danish collector, gardener, writer and photographer of geraniums Birgitte Husted Bendtsen. All four of these qualities are on show in this book based on her own personal experiences with the plants.

She has brought together a large number of different species and cultivars in her own garden, and examined and assessed them thoughtfully. She has grown them in tough conditions revealing those which are good garden plants. Her enthusiasm and experience are obvious from the tone of her writing, and her studio and garden photography, especially of the individual flowers and foliage, reveal their beauty.

This does not pretend to be an academic treatise or an exhaustive survey of the many many hundreds of *Geranium* species and cultivars which have been named. Rather this is a personal book by an enthusiast who has grown the plants. And while in the past many hardy geraniums have been looked upon almost as utilitarian plants, as solid and dependable ground covers that look after themselves, here the photographs of flowers and foliage reveal their fascinating detail and make us aware of the rewards of looking closely. Of course, the more utilitarian qualities of hardy geraniums remain valued but here another intriguing facet of their appeal is revealed.

Graham Rice

Geranium sanguineum 'Apfelblüte'

Preface

As a young garden owner and member of the Jutland Garden Society in Denmark (*Det jydske Haveselskab*), I naturally went on the garden trips organized by the society. As a rule, we west Jutlanders went eastwards. And there we found abundant lushness, fertile soil and shelter. It was always something of an anticlimax to return home again to my own garden because it suddenly seemed so small and shrivelled, almost a mummification of everything I had just seen.

"You might as well get used to it, Birgitte," said one of the other garden owners on one such trip. "When you see a plant, you just have to divide its height and width by three to work out what it would look like in our gardens."

There was definitely something in this remark—apart from one plant, which grew just as well here, in my sandy garden, as it did in those gardens with rich clay soil. This was the cranesbill, or hardy geranium. At the time, I had a bloody cranesbill, the pink 'Rose Clair' and a few others. Since then I have gradually became more and more interested in these hardy plants that grow with zeal in any conditions.

Every time I saw a new variety I bought it and now, twenty years later, I have a comprehensive collection of them. They almost never suffer problems, and are so robust that they even flourish in gardens with children and dogs—if a plant is accidentally broken, I simply cut it back and it soon flowers again. I also know from garden owners with slug and snail problems that neither of these creatures shows any interest in cranesbills.

In my garden, cranesbills flower from mid-May until well into the autumn and they have become my number one garden plant. There are many other plants in my garden, and the cranesbills are very easy to combine with them.

I would like to pass on my enthusiasm so that others can derive just as much pleasure from these delightful plants as I do. If reading this book makes just one more person want to start growing cranesbills, then I'll have achieved my goal.

Birgitte Husted Bendtsen

Family and Genus

Wild cranesbills, or geraniums, occur worldwide, mostly in temperate regions, with representatives growing in Europe, North America, South Africa, New Zealand and much of Asia. The Latin name for the cranesbill genus is *Geranium*: this is why we also call these plants geraniums, or hardy geraniums. This book often uses this designation, as the term naturally crops up in connection with the Latin names for the various varieties. The bloody cranesbill is therefore called *Geranium sanguineum* in botanical parlance. This book uses the abbreviation *G.* for *Geranium*, for example *G. sanguineum*.

Geranium means crane, and the plant's fruit resembles a crane's bill, so it is natural to call geraniums also by the common name "cranesbill".

For people, we talk about immediate families and more distant relatives. With plants, the reverse is true. We talk about a genus belonging to a family; family is the wider term. The genus *Geranium*, together with ten other genera, forms part of a family with the name Geraniaceae, the cranesbill family. In addition to cranesbills, the family includes storksbills (*Erodium*) and pelargoniums. Each genus consists of a number of species.

When is a geranium a geranium? When it's not a pelargonium

"With so many geraniums in your garden, why don't you have any bedding or rose geraniums?" This is a question I am often asked by visitors when we hold Open Garden events.

The answer is: "Because rose geraniums and bedding geraniums are pelargoniums!"

The confusion arose two hundred and fifty years ago, when Linnaeus, the Swedish

Left: The long "bill", formed once the plant has ceased flowering, has given the genus its common name of cranesbill. This is *G. macrorrhizum*, which has beautiful "bills".

8

A total of eleven genera make up the cranesbill family. Here you can see representatives of three of them. **Far left:** storksbill (*Erodium*); **left:** pelargonium; and **below:** cranesbill (*Geranium*).

Above: *G. phaeum* 'Variegatum'

botanist Carl von Linné, published his huge work on the classification of plants into genera and families. In his 1753 work, Linnaeus put cranesbills, storksbills and pelargoniums into the same genus, the genus *Geranium*. Pelargoniums come almost exclusively from South Africa, and are not winter hardy. We know them as container plants and bedding plants. In Linnaeus's time, people used bedding plants and, in particular, numerous pelargoniums in their gardens. When they talked about geraniums, they were often referring to these tender plants.

In 1789, a French amateur botanist succeeded in dividing the genus into three: *Geranium*, *Pelargonium* and *Erodium*. However, the damage was done, because although the error was rectified more than two hundred years ago, the names geranium and pelargonium still cause confusion throughout Europe.

The rose geranium is correctly called *Pelargonium graveolens*, and bedding geraniums *Pelargonium zonale*.

Species and hybrids

There are around four hundred species in the genus *Geranium*. Not all are suitable for the garden, as some are not hardy enough to

9

Above: *G. ×oxonianum* exists in many variations. 'Wageningen', shown here, has flowers of a very warm pink tone tinged with orange.

survive winter outdoors in northern climates, and others spread like weeds.

This book deals with the most common species and many of the hybrids (a hybrid has two different species as its "parents"). It would not be realistic to aim to include all the geraniums that are available. The *RHS Plant Finder 2003–2004* lists over six hundred of them from nurseries in the United Kingdom alone.

Many plant dealers regularly receive new plants from abroad, so a rare and much sought-after geranium may suddenly become available.

There are useful addresses on page 136 for your information and if you want to buy more specialist geraniums or find out about any that are completely new.

Varieties

Geranium, like other plant genera and as I mentioned on page 8, is subdivided into species. Many of the species are further split into smaller groups: subspecies; varietas, or variety; and forma. These terms are used by botanists to take into account small differences that may occur between closely related plants, such as in geographically isolated populations, or a variation in growth form or flower colour. These three terms are applied to plants found in the wild, while plants bred in cultivation are referred to as cultivars. However, in many gardening books you find the word "variety" used in a general way to cover cultivars and all the botanical terms and, as I am not a botanist, I will do the same.

Cultivation and Use

G. phaeum

G. phaeum
'Conny Broe'

G. phaeum
'Samobor'

G. cinereum Group

G. sessiliflorum
subsp. *novaezelandiae* 'Nigricans'

Soil and fertilizer

"The love of dirt is among the earliest of passions, as it is the latest. Mud-pies gratify one of our first and best instincts. As long as we are dirty, we are pure."

This is how Charles Dudley Warner, a good friend and neighbour of Mark Twain, started his gardening book *My Summer in a Garden* (1871). The type of "dirt" we become pure from messing about with is of little importance to the cranesbill. They are equally happy in light, acidic, sandy soil, clay or alkaline conditions.

When we mess about in the soil, we rediscover the creative power of our mud pie days, and cranesbills provide us with many forms and colours to play with. Their flowers are found in all shades of pink, white, blue, purple and cyclamen. In addition to the usual green, leaves may be brown or burgundy, or they may be

Above: This hardy geranium with its very attractive leaves is found in the wild. It is called *G. phaeum* 'Samobor'.

variegated with yellow, green, red and white markings. The shape and size of leaves also vary greatly.

In order to improve our very sandy soil, I add the composted manure from our four donkeys. That is all the organic matter my cranesbills get. Of course, not everyone keeps donkeys, so instead you could add another form of well-rotted organic material, such as garden compost or stable manure. As I have always been an organic gardener, I have no experience of using artificial fertilizers so I cannot make recommendations. Cranesbills are generally very easy to please and there is little need for additional feeding. However, some cranesbills, including the species that grow in very moist places in the wild, do need

Far left: Leaf section from *G. phaeum* 'Conny Broe'.

Left: A close look into *G. wallichianum* 'Buxton's Variety'.

Below left: An early spring morning when many plants, for instance the blue crocus at the top of the picture, have been struck down by a hard frost, *G. phaeum* stands upright and smart.

extra organic matter added annually to help retain the moisture in the soil. This will be noted in the text entries dealing with these slightly more demanding cranesbills.

A member of the English geranium society I belong to wrote in to the members' magazine to say she had never fertilized her garden. She only grew slug-resistant plants, and she had decided that it was the sheer frugality of cranesbills that discouraged the slugs and snails from eating them. She had noticed that it was the plants that needed a lot of fertilizer that were favoured by slugs and snails. It should also be remembered that as cranesbills are not suitable for cuttings nothing is removed, so all parts of the plants can, after dying down, be "recycled" the following year.

Planting

There is nothing special to take into consideration when planting geraniums, except for the alpine types, which are dealt with on pages 20–24. My grandfather, a keen gardener, always said: "Plant in spring and the plant may grow; plant in autumn and the plant must grow." He was referring to the warmer and moister soil conditions of autumn. However, I have heard people who garden on heavy soil complain that if they plant perennials, among them geraniums, too late in the season the plants may rot due to very wet conditions over winter. As my soil is so sandy I do not have that problem. I can plant almost when I want to, but I find it much more delightful (despite my grandfather's warning) to plant in spring because I am sooner rewarded.

Cranesbills and frost

Once the green shoots appear under the withered topgrowth of the plant, and spring has finally arrived, the days start to get longer. Subsequently we are often hit by a period of severe frost at night and stormy winds. Here in Denmark we recognize this type of weather all too well. Most cranesbills fortunately cope with it rather well. *Geranium phaeum* is tough and can put up with anything. It stands fresh, green and upright after an unseasonable frost of this type, while *G. psilostemon* and its hybrids have often lost many of their leaves. (If only winter, with its ice and snow, could just be here at the right time, and then go back to the North Pole and stay there from March to November.) In that case, we could grow a lot more plants, even if it meant we actually had a lot more frost during winter.

It is this switching between frost and mild periods that kills our plants, especially those plants that in our climate are on the borderline of being hardy. Some cranesbills of this type have started to be sold here over the last few years. *Geranium* 'Ann Folkard' and *G.* 'Salome' are two such varieties. Both have *G. procurrens* as one parent, which is not hardy in my experience.

The light pink beauty *G. ×riversleaianum* 'Mavis Simpson', which also appears in perennial catalogues, is, unfortunately, one of the less reliably hardy varieties. One of its parents is "good enough"—*G. endressii*. It is the other, from which 'Mavis Simpson' has clearly inherited its irresistible flowers, that is the problem. This other parent is called *G. traversii* and comes from New Zealand. *Geranium traversii* is a small geranium for rock gardens, and is available in two forms: one with white flowers, and one with pink flowers with a pale pink edge and dark veins. The progeny of *G. traversii* and *G. endressii* have been given the common designation *G. ×riversleaianum*. Besides 'Mavis Simpson', *G. ×riversleaianum* 'Russell Prichard', with magenta-red flowers, is also commercially available.

Of course, you may be lucky enough to enjoy these less hardy cranesbills for a number of years. When they eventually die, you can comfort yourself with the old saying: it is better to have loved and lost than never to have loved at all.

The hardy geraniums generally live for a fairly long time. Some of mine have lasted for years, and Joy Jones, chairperson of the Hardy Geranium Group in England, wrote in 2002 that she had had some of her plants since

Right: Unfortunately, this cranesbill, *G. ×riversleaianum* 'Mavis Simpson', is among the more delicate of the hardy geraniums. A characteristic of the *Geranium* genus is that the flowers occur in pairs, as shown here.

the 1960s, and that they were still in the best of health. She wonders whether the meristem-propagated plants now commercially available will be able to survive for forty years, or whether they will prove to be less stable than those propagated in the normal way.

The meristem is the name given to the type of plant tissue that can continually divide, and it is found in growth points and stems. This tissue can be used by nurseries to produce plants in test-tubes. Meristem propagation is also referred to as micro-propagation or tissue culture.

Towards the end of the book, on page 134, there is a list of other *Geranium* species not commonly grown in gardens. Where I know that a species is not hardy in my garden, I have made a note of this. If the species has not been tested, or if I do not know whether it is hardy, I have not commented on its hardiness. In these cases, a little trial and error is required. Naturally, those cranesbills that originate in very warm regions are not hardy where winters are harsh. On the other hand, you can't just assume that because a species comes from an area which experiences a lot of frost in the winter it is very hardy. It may be that the plant lies well hidden under a thick blanket of snow all winter, or that, in its natural habitat, when winter ends, it actually does end—in other words there are no alternating periods of frost and thaw.

When I have ordered new geranium hybrids from abroad, I have looked at their parentage and used a rule of thumb that if both parents are hardy, the progeny will be as well.

Care: extremely simple

This section is easy to write, as the care cranesbills require is minimal. They are, therefore, the perfect plants for beginners. The tallest plants I cut down after flowering. This kills two birds with one stone, as the plants would otherwise go to seed and also

Above: The new growth of 'Spinners', **left,** is blood red in early spring. **Right:** *G. wlassovianum*, which is completely copper-red when it breaks through the soil.

I avoid the sight of rather "tired" looking geraniums in my garden. In any case they soon flower again. The cranesbills that receive this treatment are: *G. asphodeloides*, *G. ×monacense*, *G. ×oxonianum*, *G. phaeum*, *G. pratense* and *G. sylvaticum*.

Disease is also an easy subject to deal with: *G. pratense* suffers from mildew in some years, but this can be dealt with by cutting back.

The only virus I have read about that can be found in cranesbills has not bothered mine. It affects those geraniums from warmer climates such as *G. canariense*, and a few

others I do not have, as they are not hardy.

In the wild, the habitats of the various *Geranium* species vary from woods to sunny mountainsides. There are, therefore, cranesbills suitable for every type of garden. It is almost as if they do their best to adapt to their habitat, although this may not be absolutely by the book. Naturally, this does not mean that you can go to extremes and expect a small rock garden species to flourish in a woodland bed.

The huge variety of cranesbills provides a multitude of options for use in the garden.

Green Leaves

G. ×cantabrigiense

G. cinereum Group

G. 'Purple Pillow'

G. clarkei

G. himalayense

G. gracile

G. macrorrhizum

G. 'Nimbus'

G. ×magnificum

G. nodosum

G. ×oxonianum

G. phaeum

G. ×oxonianum

G. pratense

G. renardii

G. psilostemon

G. renardii

G. sanguineum

G. sylvaticum

G. 'Tiny Monster'

Leaves with Dark Markings

G. pratense
Midnight Reiter

G. ×oxonianum
'Dawn Time'

G. maculatum
'Espresso'

G. ×oxonianum
'Katherine Adele'

G. ×monacense
'Muldoon'

G. phaeum 'Samobor'

G. sessiliflorum subsp.
novaezelandiae 'Nigricans'

G. sessiliflorum subsp.
novaezelandiae 'Porter's Pass'

G. wlassovianum

G. phaeum 'Margaret Wilson'

Leaves with Yellow Markings

G. 'Anne Thomson'

G. 'Ann Folkard'

G. 'Blue Sunrise'

G. orientali-tibeticum

G. phaeum 'Lisa'

G. macrorrhizum 'Variegatum'

G. phaeum
'Margaret Wilson'

G. phaeum 'Conny Broe'

G. thunbergii
'Jester's Jacket'

G. phaeum 'Variegatum'

G. phaeum 'Taff's Jester'

Hardy Geraniums for Rock Gardens

"It's a sobering thought to consider what a grower of alpine plants hopes to achieve," said author and designer Duncan Lowe during a lecture to members of the Alpine Garden Society, a club for growers of alpine plants in the United Kingdom. He was referring to the immense changes in living conditions alpine plants are subjected to when they are planted in gardens. "And if these poor confused plants eventually succumb, they are described as hard to please," continued Lowe in his lecture, as quoted in the society's newsletter.

This group of plants, which we rather unfairly judge to be difficult, also includes certain cranesbills, namely those described as alpine geraniums. These are almost exclusively cranesbills belonging to the Cinereum Group (see page 52). Strictly speaking, a plant is described as an alpine if it grows in the Alps, but the expression is used more broadly and generally refers to plants that grow at high altitudes in mountainous regions.

The living conditions there are very specific and difficult. A fresh wind blows high up on the mountainside where there are no trees to offer shelter. It is important, therefore, for plants not to poke out of the ground too much, to prevent their delicate parts being buffeted about or too much water evaporating from the stems and leaves. Therefore, large, lush cranesbills are not normally found on mountaintops, but small hairy plants, whose flower stems run along the ground, are. The ground is, of course, very stony, so the plants dry out very quickly after a rain shower, and mould and fungus are unable to take hold. The light is intense so photosynthesis is unrestricted, something which is necessary due to the short growing season. The plants "down on lower ground" have from March to October to grow and set seed, whereas alpine plants only have three months for this. For them, the light suddenly disappears when winter arrives in the mountains. A blanket of snow is thrown over the alpine plants, so they can

Above: *Geranium gymnocaulon* can grow in rock gardens. Here it is planted between a red and blue *Prunella*.

Above and below: *G.* 'Purple Pillow' is a completely different shade of red from the other geraniums in the Cinereum Group.

sleep well and stay warm until spring comes.

When these alpine plants are grown in gardens, we cannot give them the peace to "hibernate". The weather is a constant tease; one day it is mild and the plants start growing, the next it is frosty again. It's tough for them.

Cultivation

So, what can we do to help small alpine geraniums grow and flourish in the rock garden?

Naturally, they should be planted where they can get plenty of light and air, so a sunny spot is vital. We have no control over the winter weather, but we can ensure that the plants never become waterlogged. If the plants are constantly wet, they are attacked by mould and fungus. The most important thing when growing alpine plants is to ensure the plants have a free-draining situation, with no chance of them becoming waterlogged. To this end, place a top dressing of stone chippings or gravel around the root collars of the plant. Also ensure good drainage by adding coarse sand and gravel to the soil so water runs through quickly.

When I began growing rock plants, I thought it was necessary to protect them from water as much as possible. I therefore avoided watering them in dry summers when I used the sprinkler on other plants in the garden. I now know this was a waste of time, as alpine plants like water during the growing season. It is winter rainfall that causes such catastrophic results.

Alpine plants grow in a medium that contains plenty of oxygen. The coarse drainage material we add to the soil or compost is therefore important for creating an open structure so the air can circulate and oxygen can penetrate. However, what the alpine plants' natural growing medium

Right: Fear of heights is no obstacle to growing alpine plants. Alpine cranesbills are perfectly content on walls and slopes, even though they only grow a few centimetres above the ground.

Right: *G. sessiliflorum* subsp. *novaezelandiae* 'Nigricans' naturally has very light-coloured flowers, as it comes from New Zealand (see page 119).

Far right: *G. bohemicum* is an annual, so I hope it seeds.

does not have a lot of is nitrogen. They can, therefore, easily be overfed in gardens.

One habitat preferred by many alpine plants is any place where the rock has become weathered and is so porous or fragile that it has become pulverized. Here, the content of soluble minerals and trace elements is high, which is why we must conclude that these modest alpine plants, despite everything, actually do have something to live on.

According to Duncan Lowe, a tried and tested soil mixture for alpines is made up of three parts by volume coarse sand, consisting of 3–5 mm particles, to one part leafmould.

The Rock Garden

When you grow alpine geraniums, you don't need to build huge mountains for the plants. Alpines in the garden do not need to be raised above 25 cm, so all you need is a raised bed. The easiest thing to do is to put soil mixed with coarse sand in the spot where you want to create the bed. Of course, the location must be cleared first and should not contain any perennial weeds such as ground elder or similar. However, the raised bed can contain attractive pieces of rock or stones.

I believe plants and stone complement each other, and large stones or rocks provide excellent growing conditions for alpines. In dry periods, the roots can find moisture under a large stone, and the stones can provide non-absorbent surfaces for the plant's stems and leaves to rest on.

Make sure that you can't see the base of a large stone or rock in the bed. If you can, you lose the illusion that it is actually bedrock that is exposed in your garden. It is very difficult to get large, round stones to lie neatly, so try to avoid using them when building a rock garden.

If, for one reason or another, you do not want a rock garden or raised bed in the garden, you can grow alpine geraniums in troughs or pots. Naturally, excellent drainage is also required here. Some people

Above: *G. subcaulescens* 'Splendens' dates from 1930.
Below: *G. ×lindavicum* 'Apple Blossom' is beautiful, but difficult as it is one of the alpine cranesbills.

Above: By placing a layer of gravel under alpine plants and around the root collars, you can provide the plants with the rapidly draining conditions they need in the fight against mould and fungus.

Right: *G.* 'Kahlua' has the combination of delicate pink flowers and dark leaves that so many of us find irresistible.

cover alpine plants with a pane of glass or similar in the winter to protect them from winter rain. I have never done this, and consequently I have lost a few plants now and then after particularly wet, harsh winters. I take this in my stride.

Plant neighbours for the small alpine geraniums must naturally be suitable for rock gardens, for example *Dianthus* (pinks) or *Sedum* (stonecrops). If you become seriously interested in rock plants, the Alpine Garden Society can supply excellent help and advice (see Address List).

Non-alpine geraniums for the rock garden

Geraniums in the Cinereum Group and *G. farreri* are plants that require special handling as described above in the instructions for growing alpine plants. However, there is a huge difference in how difficult or "alpine" these geraniums are. By far the easiest to grow are the varieties of *G. subcaulescens* and hybrids between this species and *G. cinereum*. The popular 'Ballerina' is one of these hybrids.

However, there are many geraniums that do not need to grow in a rock garden at all, but are definitely suitable for one. Because they are so small, they may be overwhelmed by other plants growing in herbaceous borders. *Geranium dalmaticum* is a good example of such a geranium. There may also

Right: *G. sanguineum* var. *striatum* is an utterly unique geranium. It is only found growing wild in one place in the world, in Cumbria, England. It comes true from seed and is unashamedly pretty, both in its flowers and its foliage.

given last spring, is a hybrid of this type, so I must just enjoy it for as long as I have it.

Some of the small geraniums suitable for rock gardens can cope with almost anything. I am thinking of species that run amok with rhizomes and tubers. These include *G. pylzowianum*, *G. orientali-tibeticum*, and *G. tuberosum*. If these species are planted in the middle of a rock garden, they can be very difficult to manage, as they shoot up everywhere, and you can't dig between the stones or you will destroy something else. Therefore plant these species at the edge of your rock garden or in a pot. *Geranium orientali-tibeticum* has abundant attractive, mottled yellow and green leaves. *Geranium pylzowianum* has very fine leaves and pink flowers with cream-coloured stamens. *Geranium tuberosum* has attractive bluish purple flowers with dark veins early in the season. Considering the excellent characteristics of these plants, it is even more annoying that they behave as they do.

In this section of the book, it has not been my intention to catalogue all cranesbills that can grow in rock gardens. It is a question of taste whether you want to plant, for example, the taller varieties of *G. sanguineum*, *G. phaeum* or *G. ×magnificum* in your rock garden. They can easily cope. I hope, however, that I have given an indication of the growing conditions required for cranesbills that can only grow in rock gardens.

The encyclopaedic section of the book contains other cranesbills suitable for rock gardens and more information on those already mentioned.

Where a rock garden and ordinary borders sit side by side, I plant cranesbills that are suitable for both situations. These include *G. macrorrhizum*, which in the wild grows in the mountains of southern Europe, and taller varieties of *G. sanguineum*.

The small cranesbills for rock gardens arouse roughly the same feelings in me as when I see a puppy—they are just so appealing. And, the best thing about them is that I can grow so many in a small area.

be specific features, such as very hairy leaves, that make certain plants particularly suited to the conditions in rock gardens. These include *G. renardii* and its hybrids, such as *G.* 'Philippe Vapelle' and *G.* 'Stephanie.'

I myself have many variations of *G. sanguineum* in my rock garden. In my opinion, the lowest growing varieties are the ones that work best, such as 'Apfelblüte', 'Shepherd's Warning', 'Jubilee Pink', 'Canon Miles', and *G. sanguineum* var. *striatum*.

A single annual has been allowed in this year. It is *G. bohemicum*, which has very beautiful blue flowers. I hope it seeds (but

moderately) so I can enjoy it again next year. To be on the safe side, I'll collect some seeds from it and save them. Another geranium that only survives in my garden through saved seeds is *G. cataractarum*, which has bright orange stamens and deep pink flowers.

Although the brown-leaved New Zealander, *G. sessiliflorum* subsp. *novae-zelandiae* 'Nigricans' is not completely hardy, it is excellent at seeding. There are a number of hybrids of this geranium and its non-hardy "countryman", *G. traversii*, available for the rock garden. These hybrids have brown leaves and pale pink flowers. I would guess that *G.* 'Kahlua', which I was

Above: A pink *G. ×oxonianum* forms a base for the Alba rose 'Celestial'. (Photograph: Lene Juhl Jørgensen)

Hardy Geraniums and Roses

By Lene Juhl Jørgensen, guest writer and landscape gardener

Roses and hardy geraniums are made for each other. In a romantic garden with old-fashioned shrub roses, beds with fragrant English roses and lush climbing roses, geraniums, with their fine green leaves, are ideal for covering the ground. The small, charming flowers of the geraniums provide relief among the roses' full, heavy heads.

When selecting geraniums for your roses, however, you must take into account whether their height, colour and flowering times are complementary.

Match growth and habit

Hardy geraniums that form low cushions or carpets are fine for edging rose beds. The height of these geraniums must be considered and not exceed the height and growth rate of the roses, so the roses will not be smothered. On the other hand, tall geraniums can easily be planted behind and between rose bushes, so their flowers will be on a level with the roses.

Geranium sanguineum var. *striatum*, *G. ×riversleaianum* 'Mavis Simpson', *G. wallichianum* and *G. renardii* are all suitable cranesbills for planting in front of low, slow-growing roses. If rose bushes are around a metre high, *G. sanguineum* and its various magenta and white varieties will look very attractive in the foreground.

To cover the ground in front of taller rose bushes and climbers, the selection of geraniums can be extended to include the blue *G. himalayense* and *G.* 'Johnson's Blue', the pink *G. endressii* and the long-flowering *G. ×oxonianum,* and definitely the short-flowering *G. ×magnificum* and *G. clarkei* 'Kashmir White.'

As a background and for interplanting, varieties of the tall *G. pratense*, *G.* 'Brookside' and *G. psilostemon* are ideal, as they begin flowering at the start of the rose season.

Match flowering times and colours

The old-fashioned roses, as a rule, flower from the end of June for three weeks. Most cranesbills also flower in this period, so it is easy to find good ones to complement the old roses. If you want to pair flowering cranesbills with roses that bloom for longer, such as English roses and remontant roses such as the Portland roses, Bourbon roses and musk roses, you need to choose from the longer-flowering cranesbills, such as *G. ×oxonianum*, *G. ×riversleaianum* and *G. wallichianum*. *Geranium* 'Johnson's Blue' and certain varieties of *G. sanguineum* may also repeat flower. Early tall-growing geraniums such as *G. phaeum* and *G. sylvaticum* normally flower before roses, but can thus be used to provide earlier interest in the background of rose beds.

The low, ground-covering geraniums *G. macrorrhizum* and *G. ×cantabrigiense* also

flower before roses, but their close leaves form a fine, green base in the shade of tall rose bushes and climbers. If you choose geraniums that bloom at the same time as roses, you need to consider their respective flower colours, and to what extent they should complement each other.

White roses

All colours of geranium complement a white rose. You can achieve a poetic atmosphere by combining white roses with light blue cranesbills. The white English rose **Winchester Cathedral** ('Auscat'), flanked by *G. pratense* 'Mrs Kendall Clark' with its light blue, white-veined flowers and *G. pratense* 'Wisley Blue', with the loveliest lavender-blue flowers, is an enchanting sight. 'Mrs Kendall Clark' flowers for a relatively short time in late June, while 'Wisley Blue' flowers for most of July. A

blue base of *G. himalayense* and the late summer flowering *G. wallichianum* 'Buxton's Variety' in front of the rose completes the picture.

Another good combination of white and blue is the tall, white Alba rose 'Madame Plantier' with light blue *G.* 'Johnson's Blue'.

If you want a pure white rose bed in the garden, white cranesbills such as *G. sanguineum* 'Album', *G. clarkei* 'Kashmir White', *G. clarkei* 'Kashmir Green' and *G. ×oxonianum* 'Ankum's White' can be combined with white roses. However, only the first three flower at the start of the rose season, while *G. ×oxonianum* 'Ankum's White' flowers for the whole season. This variety can be supplemented with later perennials with white flowers or grey leaves.

Pink roses

Blue and violet-flowered cranesbills and pink roses create an attractive tableau. But combining various shades of pink roses and cranesbills can also be beautiful. You only need to distinguish between the cool pink shades with blue tones and the warm pink

shades with yellow tones. Many of the old-fashioned rose bushes have cool pink blooms. A fine combination in cool tones is the Bourbon rose 'Reine Victoria' in a base of mixed *G. ×oxonianum* varieties such as 'Bregover Pearl', 'Old Rose', 'Rebecca Moss' and 'Phoebe Noble'. A different and lower-growing base in front of old garden roses with cool pink colours may be *G. sanguineum* 'Cedric Morris' with its large magenta flowers.

Modern low roses may also have purplish pink blooms. This is true, for instance, of **Bewitched** ('Poulbella'), which is attractive in a base of the low-growing and barely hardy *G. ×riversleaianum* 'Mavis Simpson', which flowers abundantly for long periods in late summer. Why not add greyish leaves from *G. renardii* and perhaps lamb's ears (*Stachys byzantina*)to the base?

Warm pink tones are found in many modern roses, including the ground-covering varieties. A combination of delicate pink colours could be the ground-covering rose **Little Bo Peep** ('Poullen') and the low-growing cranesbill *G. sanguineum* var. *striatum*. Warm pink tones are also found in some old roses such as the Alba rose

Above: The apothecary's rose, *Rosa gallica* var. *officinalis*, in a purple-coloured bed with *G. sanguineum* and *Salvia nemorosa* 'Ostfriesland'.

Left: *G. sanguineum* 'Cedric Morris' as a base planting under an unidentified old shrub rose.

(Photographs: Lene Juhl Jørgensen)

'Maiden's Blush', which matches the colour of *G.* ×*oxonianum* 'Wargrave Pink'.

Carmine and purple roses

If you prefer strong and dramatic colours, you can plant carmine and purple-coloured roses together with cranesbills in shades of magenta and violet. A bed of Gallica roses such as the carmine-coloured *Rosa gallica* var. *officinalis* and the dark purple 'Hippolyte' supplemented with the rambler 'Bleu Magenta' will look fantastic with a base of magenta *G. sanguineum*, interplanted with the double violet *G. pratense* 'Plenum Violaceum'. Small clusters of the dark violet *Salvia nemorosa* 'Ostfriesland' between the geraniums will match the colours in the purple bed.

Yellow and peach-coloured roses

Yellows are not found among the old roses, but some tall rose bushes such as Burnet rose hybrids have yellow or peach-coloured blooms, as do many English roses. Blue cranesbills give a fresh touch to light yellow and peach-coloured roses. If you want a softer, more delicate effect, white cranesbills such as *G. sanguineum* 'Album' form an excellent base, which also works well with warm yellow roses.

Above: The Bourbon rose 'Reine Victoria' grows in a base of pearly everlasting and *G.* ×*oxonianum* 'Old Rose' and 'Bregover Pearl', with the low-growing 'Frank Lawley' in the foreground.

(Photograph: Lene Juhl Jørgensen)

Hardy Geraniums and Bees

Above: The style and stamens form a pillar that the bee can cling to for the three seconds or so that it is in the geranium flower. (Photograph: John Brackenbury, University of Cambridge)

Right: Here, we are so close that you can see the entrance to the "honey pots", the nectaries that sit between the petals. Only three of the stamens in this flower are intact. Among the species with large flowers which are designed for pollination by insects, the flower has a male stage and a female stage. When the pollen grains are mature (male stage) the stigma is not ready to receive pollen. When the stigma is ready, the flower is in the female stage. This division, which is called protandry, encourages cross-pollination.
(Photograph: John Brackenbury, University of Cambridge)

Pollination

A bright summer day, with bees buzzing around the cranesbills, fills me with great joy: "I have planted something someone can use!"

The bee lingers in the cranesbill flower for a little under three seconds. It sticks its proboscis into the "honey pots" of nectar and deposits the pollen on the stigma, so the flower can be fertilized and form seeds.

The bee flies from cranesbill to cranesbill. Fortunately, it does not fly at random—from a rose to a cranesbill and perhaps on to a salvia. If that were to happen, seeds would rarely result from pollination. It is said that bees are "loyal" to their flowers. It is the more highly developed flowers, including the majority of garden cranesbills, that have this incredible relationship with bees: the bees pollinate the flowers, and the work is "paid for" with nectar and pollen. When and where the agreement was made

is a mystery, or as Darwin called it, "a detestable mystery".

I am sure that this cooperation began here where I live in West Jutland, as for both parties it is a question of whether or not it is worth it. The flower tries to get by as cheaply as possible, as producing nectar requires a huge amount of energy. The bee, on the other hand, will not fly after nectar if there is no benefit—if it costs more energy to collect it than it gains.

The flower must hide the nectar (the bait) well, so that passing insects cannot snatch it without real intent. However, if the hiding place is too difficult to find, and the nectar is almost inaccessible, this is a setback for the flower, as the bee will simply not be bothered to find the treasure and will fly past. Among members of the *Geranium* genus, the nectar is hidden at the base of the flower, between the five petals in five so-called "nectaries".

In order to make access for the bees easier, the geranium flowers have ensured good parking conditions while bees are working (see photograph above). This is the pillar in the centre of the flower, to which the bee can easily cling. It consists of the style with the stigma at the top, which is divided into five parts, and the stamens.

The stamens, each made up of a filament and pollen-bearing anther, sit in two rings surrounding the style. Each ring has five stamens. The number five is repeated in the number of sepals. The sepals are the green

Nectary—or "honey pot"

Style

Stigma

Ovary

Filament

Anther

Stamen

Below: Here the seeds have just been flung out into the world by means of the spring device. Taxonomist Peter Yeo (see page 33) divides the *Geranium* species into three types, corresponding to these three ways the seeds can be ejected:
1 As illustrated in the picture below, where the seed is thrown from the fruit compartment, and the empty fruit compartment and the coiled up part of the bill are left behind.

2 The fruit compartment stays with the seed, and the bill section falls off.
3 The fruit compartment and bill section stay with the seed.

Above: The fruit compartments can be seen at the bottom of the "bill". The ovary is divided into five compartments attached to the bill, but these compartments are not connected to each other.

leaves on the outside of the flower, which protect the petals and the inner parts of the flower while it is in bud (see photograph on page 29, which shows the individual parts of the flower). The flowers almost always occur in pairs.

Many geraniums have stripes on their petals and these show the bee how to get to the nectar. Examples include *G. nodosum*, *G. renardii* and *G. gracile*, which all have well-defined stripes.

A bee must consume 10 milligrams of sugar an hour to be able to keep flying. If the bee is too far away from home for it to return before darkness falls, or it does not have enough "fuel" for its journey back, it must find a place to stay overnight. The geranium flower offers excellent accommodation. You can see two bees in the picture opposite sharing a "double room". We know that bees can easily remember the following day which type of flower they were working on, so the next morning these two bees will continue with geraniums.

Fruit and seeds

As soon as the geranium has been pollinated, the top of the ovary begins to grow so that the style with the stigma begins to poke right out of the flower. In this way, the characteristic cranesbill is formed, constituting a spring-like device to spread the seeds properly, so that the progeny can get out into the world and colonize it.

The ovary is divided into five small

Above: The lines on the petals are guides that lead insects to the nectar. The flower shown is *G. gracile*.

compartments, each of which, as a rule, contains a seed. Each of the five compartments is tightly attached to the "bill" at the top, but they are not connected to each other. When the seeds are mature, the bill shrivels up and five strips, each with a fruit compartment at the bottom end, peel off the core. With enormous power the fruit compartments shoot outwards, as the strips coil up like springs at the same time as the seeds are thrown out (see photograph).

Geranium renardii

Below: You almost want to place a little blanket over the two bees curled up together and asleep in this cranesbill flower. The picture is from the book *Insects and Flowers* (1995), which I was very taken with. I managed to contact the author, John Brackenbury, who works at the Department of Anatomy at the University of Cambridge, England, and was given permission to use the picture. (Photograph: John Brackenbury, University of Cambridge)

Geranium pratense 'Mrs Kendall Clark'

Species and Hybrids

Isn't it amazing that bees can definitely distinguish between a geranium and a salvia, or another flower in the garden, when I consider how long it took me to learn to recognise the most common garden plants?

But bees do not always distinguish between species within the same genus. So a bee may transfer pollen from one species to another, making it possible for two species of cranesbill to be crossed with one another and form a hybrid. If the hybrid is found in a garden where several species of geranium grow, you cannot know which are the "parents". If a plant has appeared in a group of self-sown geraniums, perhaps you can tell which is the "mother" but not the "father". Such hybrids are therefore simply called *Geranium* followed by a name that says nothing of the species involved, for example *Geranium* 'Spinners' or *G*. 'Ann Folkard'. The name can be chosen by the owner of the plant or the nursery launching the plant.

In a few individual cases, where two species often cross, botanists have chosen to give the progeny a common "surname". You then call the seedlings *Geranium* × one or another name that has been adopted, which refers to the relevant crossed species. For example, it has been decided that all geraniums that have *G. versicolor* and *G. endressii* as parents are to be called *G.* ×*oxonianum* (see page 93). One of the most common cranesbills in Danish gardens is of this type, namely *G.* ×*oxonianum* 'Rose Clair'.

Geranium versicolor and *G. endressii* will, when planted close to each other, have many "children" together. It is questionable whether it is possible to purchase pure species of these two geraniums. In any case, it is pretty certainly an oxonianum geranium that hides behind the name *G. endressii* at nurseries. *Geranium sanguineum*, the bloody cranesbill, on the other hand, almost never crosses with other species. This is because *G. sanguineum* has

84 chromosomes, whereas the majority of other geraniums have 28.

In nature, the obstacle in forming hybrids is not just a difference in the number of chromosomes. There is often what we call a geographical obstacle due to the fact that species grow on opposite sides of the world. In the garden, things are a little different. Here, we have plants from North America growing next to plants from the Himalayas. Many hybrids have thus been created in gardens.

However, many of the hybrids are sterile and cannot form seeds. A familiar example is *G*. 'Johnson's Blue', which for the same reason flowers for a long period. It constantly "waits" for pollination and fertilization and continues to form flowers.

In order to see which species are closely related to each other, scientists, particularly at the University of Cambridge, England, have tried to cross many different species of *Geranium*. Nursery people and gardeners have also worked on the same task, but here the aim has been to create good garden plants. As a taxonomist at the University Botanic Garden, Cambridge, Peter Yeo, has worked on the classification of the genus *Geranium*. He has written up the work in his book *Hardy Geraniums* (see Bibliography, page 137).

A gardener in the Isles of Orkney, Scotland, has become world famous for his geranium hybrids. His name is Alan Bremner, and from him we have *G*. 'Anne Thomson', *G*. ×*cantabrigiense* 'St. Ola', *G*. 'Chantilly', *G*. 'Natalie' and *G*. 'Patricia', among others (see photographs, right).

The individual species of *Geranium* often vary in the wild. A species that generally has cyclamen red flowers may suddenly pop up in the wild in a version with white or pink flowers. When plants that are deviations of a species are cultivated, they are given the species name followed by a registered cultivar name, for example *G. sanguineum* 'Cedric Morris' or *G. himalayense* 'Irish Blue'.

Geranium 'Anne Thomson'

Geranium 'Chantilly'

Geranium 'Patricia'

Geranium ×*cantabrigiense* 'St. Ola'

Above: A gardener in the Orkney Islands Alan Bremner, has become world famous for his geranium hybrids. From him we have, among others, *G*. 'Anne Thomson', *G*. ×*cantabrigiense* 'St. Ola', *G*. 'Chantilly', *G*. 'Natalie' and *G*. 'Patricia'.

Geranium phaeum 'Chocolate Chip'

Propagating Hardy Geraniums

1 The seeds are large enough that they can be easily spaced over the compost surface. Remember to note down the name of the seeds you have sown.

2 The seeds should be gently pushed in contact with the compost. Then I cover them with diatomaceous earth because it is easy to see whether the seeds are moist by its colour, but you could use grit.

3 This is what it looks like when the seeds sprout. Soon something more interesting will appear between the seed leaves.

Your garden will never look better than it will next year! By then, you will have planted even more of your favourite flowers. You also know just how you want the garden to look. Most cranesbills are easy to propagate, so you can have as many of your favourites as you want.

Some cranesbills can be sown to produce plants with the same genes as the mother plant. These are described as coming true to seed. Hybrids are never true to seed. Their progeny's genes vary, so some plants resemble one of the hybrid's parents, some the other, while others resemble the hybrid itself. It is said that the progeny have split. In many cases hybrids are sterile, which means they do not form seeds. It could also be that the hybrid does form seeds, which germinate, but the progeny are unable to survive.

Sowing

Geranium seeds are wonderfully large, so they can be handled individually. I get seeds from the various societies I belong to, or from some of the larger seed firms (see Address List at the back of the book). Naturally, you can also harvest your own seeds in your garden.

I sow the seeds in February, and the pots are left outside in all types of weather; after all in the wild there is nobody to bring them in. I use large pots to make sure that the seeds do not dry out if I don't attend to them for a while. As the seeds should not be soaking wet the whole time either, I make sure there is plenty of drainage in the pots to prevent them from rotting. The seed compost, which I buy in bags, is mixed with horticultural sand, grit or vermiculite, or I use diatomaceous earth. Around a quarter of the seed compost is drainage material. Remember to make a note of what you have sown in the pot; you never remember as well as you think. I myself write on the pot itself so there is nothing to be blown away, as sometimes happens with a label.

In order to prevent birds picking at the pots, I place a net over them. I use one of the fine nets that protect my carrots against carrot fly in summer. Once the seedlings have developed their first permanent leaves, after the seed leaves, you can transplant them.

Some seeds are unwilling to sprout. You can help them on their way by cutting a small hole in the thickest end of the seed with nail clippers. The hard seed shells will then be permeable to water, which starts the process of germination.

As already mentioned, hybrids are never true to seed, but if you restrict yourself to sowing species, you can generally count on getting seedlings that are of the same species as the plant that supplied the seeds. Although you can be virtually assured that, for example, you will get a himalayense geranium when you sow seeds from *G. himalayense* 'Gravetye' or another variety of *G. himalayense*, be aware that there is a chance you will get a new, exciting hybrid.

Often you can identify hybrids as early as

Below left: *G. pratense* 'Striatum' is barely true to seed, but at this stage you cannot see if the progeny will have the attractive lavender-blue patches of the mother plant. However, when the first leaf stems appear, you can then tell from their colour: if they are reddish, then the plant has not inherited the patches, but if the leaf stems are light green you have a *G. pratense* 'Striatum'.

Above: Take basal cuttings before the leaves unfold completely. A plant that does not need to be dug up soon gets over this interference. Here basal cuttings are being cut from *G. pratense* 'Striatum' on 14 April.

the pricking out stage, as many differ from their siblings in the pot by having yellow or variegated leaves.

Examples of geraniums that easily form hybrids are *G. endressii* and *G. versicolor*. Where these species are found growing close to one other, you cannot count on getting either species true through sowing. Other examples of geraniums that sometimes form hybrids with each other are *G. phaeum* and *G. reflexum*, and similarly *G. pratense* can cross with *G. collinum* or *G. clarkei*. *Geranium traversii* and *G. argenteum* also cross easily with *G. ×oxonianum* and *G. cinereum* respectively.

Division and basal cuttings

Most geraniums are easy to divide into smaller pieces with green tops and roots, just as we split other perennials. A perennial geranium has a rhizome with roots. New leaves will push through from this rhizome in spring. Some geraniums, for example *G. pratense* and *G. psilostemon*, have thick and woody rhizomes and roots so the plants are difficult to divide. For these you can use a

different method. You can take cuttings from low down, in the soil, when the plant has just broken through. These cuttings are known as basal cuttings. Cut off a new shoot just below the soil surface using a sharp knife. The plant does not need to be lifted, so this method causes minimal damage.

The basal cuttings are potted and kept moist. Do not place them in direct sunlight, but protect them in a greenhouse, a cold frame or under a plastic cover. Remember in the latter case to ensure the cuttings get plenty of ventilation to prevent them from rotting. After three to five weeks, the cuttings will have developed roots.

Sometimes you may be lucky enough to get a shoot with a little root on it. An idiot-proof cutting of this kind is known as an "Irishman's cutting".

Underground stems

In certain cases geraniums spread by means of rhizomes that extend horizontally underground, and often store nutrients for the plant. The rhizomes also have buds from which new shoots can develop.

Below: The basal cuttings are potted up and kept moist. Three to five weeks later, you will have fine, new plants.

Many cranesbills have such horizontal rhizomes, and this type of cranesbill is very easy to propagate. You only need to take a piece of the rhizome and pot it, but you must make sure that the piece has a bud.

You should not take too small a piece, as there will not be enough nutrients to sustain a new plant, The thinner the rhizome, the longer the piece you need to use. A 7–8 cm length is necessary from *G. himalayense*, for example, while *G. phaeum* has such thick rhizomes that less is required.

The picture at the top of the page shows various types of rhizomes. *Geranium phaeum* has very thick rhizomes that lie just below the surface of the soil, while *G. himalayense* has long, thin rhizomes. *Geranium sanguineum* has highly budded rhizomes, and *G. macrorrhizum* produces many rhizomes above the ground.

In some plants, sections of the rhizomes can be exceedingly swollen with nutrients. These swollen sections are called tubers. Some geraniums form tubers, for example *G. tuberosum* (tuberosum refers precisely to these tubers). In such cases you can get new plants just by potting the tubers.

Root cuttings

Some plants have roots that are remarkable in their ability to produce buds and turn into new plants. We are all too familiar with this ability in thistles, but actually very few plants can accomplish this trick.

Above: 1 *G. phaeum* has thick, brittle rhizomes that are easy to break into pieces.
2 Sometimes a small amount of root comes away with the basal cutting. Here is *G.* 'Patricia' supplying such an "Irishman's cutting".

Above: 3 *G. orientali-tibeticum*, the lowest part of which can be seen in the picture, is one of those geraniums with tubers.
4 *G. subcaulescens* 'Splendens' is so small that it was easiest to pull up a clump to take basal cuttings.

1 Early in the spring, just before growth starts, you can take root cuttings from geraniums in the Cinereum Group. This is G. 'Laurence Flatman'. Wash the soil from the roots so you can see them properly to select the best ones.

2 Cut the roots into sections around 4 cm long using a sharp, clean knife or razor blade.

3 Pot up the root cuttings in the same mixture recommended for sowing (see page 35). Make sure the cuttings are the same way up as they were when they were part of the root, with the top just visible. Cover the compost surface with a drainage layer of horticultural sand. Keep the cuttings moist, but not soaking wet.

Above: After two to three weeks, a small green ring will appear at the top of the cutting, which is a good sign. Soon a leaf will push through. I have tried this propagation method a few times with varying success.

Geraniums in the Cinereum Group can be propagated by using sections of the root (see illustrations). Make sure these sections of root are inserted the same way up as they were when they were part of the root system. Pot up the pieces vertically so that the top part, which on the plant was closest to the stems, is level with the soil surface. Stand the pots in a warm place, indoors or in a greenhouse.

Root cuttings must be taken just before growth starts in the spring, some time around the beginning of March would be best in most regions. If you leave this too late, the plant will have used its strength to sprout out new leaves. Geraniums in the Cinereum Group can also, and more easily, be propagated using basal cuttings.

I have read that you can also propagate G. pratense by means of root cuttings, but I myself have never had any success using this method.

Leaf from *G. sanguineum*

Below: *Geranium sanguineum* 'Shooting Star' is the result of Rolf Offenthal from Germany crossing *G. sanguineum* 'Elsbeth' and *G. sanguineum* 'Shepherd's Warning'.

What about ordinary stem cuttings?

One summer I tried to see if it was possible to propagate geraniums using cuttings in the same way as you can with pelargoniums—you just take a piece of stem with leaves and pot it up. I wondered why I could get cuttings from some geraniums, for example *G. wallichianum* and *G. sanguineum*, to produce roots in this way, while cuttings from other geraniums, such as *G. ×oxonianum*, refused to do so.

Now I know why.

In spring, when the geranium's rhizome produces a new leaf, this leaf sits like a rosette on the rhizome. The rosette and rhizome are designed to live for a long time. They form the plant's perennial part. The stems that are subsequently sent out over the ground are designed to carry the flowers, which only survive the summer or for a single season. These flower-bearing stems are therefore not able to put down roots for a longer stay. Thus flower stems of *G. ×oxonianum* and many other geraniums do not produce roots.

In *G. sanguineum* and *G. wallichianum* the rhizome sends out only a few, if any, leaves in spring. The permanent leaves do not sit in a rosette on the rhizome, but on the flower stems, which therefore have the ability to live for a long time and produce roots. We can thus propagate these geraniums by means of stem cuttings. *Geranium sanguineum*, however, is so easy to propagate using rhizomes that it is hardly worth using the stem cuttings method.

When it comes to *G. wallichianum* (especially 'Buxton's Variety'), which is extremely difficult to divide, it is very fortunate that you can just pot a piece of stem and get it to put down roots. I have read that *G.* 'Ann Folkard' can also be propagated using stem cuttings, so obviously I will have to try this propagation method on my latest geranium, *G.* 'Blue Sunrise', which is a cross between 'Ann Folkard' and *G. wallichianum*.

A Visit to Coen Jansen

A name you often come across when reading about geraniums is Coen Jansen. He is a nurseryman and author of the book *Geranium für den Garten* (*Geraniums for your garden*—see Bibliography, page 137). Coen Jansen lives in Dalfsen, near Zwolle, in northeastern Holland.

I have many cranesbills created or introduced by Coen Jansen in my garden, so it was with huge expectations that I went to visit Coen in July 2003, together with Vita Balle from Forlaget Geranium.

Coen Jansen's nursery is extremely well equipped. There is a huge number of plants, but everything is organized and well planned. An area in the centre, covered by a lawn, provides light and space. On one side the plants for sale are arranged along wide flagged paths. On the other side is Coen's

garden containing many of the parent plants. The time of my visit coincided with the point in the growing season when plants tend to be thoroughly tired of being in pots, so it was astounding to see such healthy plants in the sweltering heat.

Besides geraniums, Coen Jansen also has many other plants. Late summer perennials such as loosestrife, helenium and perennial phlox stood in full flower between *Heuchera* (alum roots) with every conceivable leaf colour. Light and dark blue agapanthus sat in huge pots. A swarm of butterflies fluttered around the many types of *Agastache*; these were Coen's sterile versions that obviously, nevertheless, produced plenty of nectar.

Above: A view over Coen Jansen's nursery, which is extremely well equipped.

Hardy geraniums from Coen Jansen

The plants growing for sale the following year extend over a large area, covered with shade nets. Many new geranium varieties have "found their feet" here at this nursery; varieties that have arisen as accidental, but unique, seedlings either at the nursery, or in the gardens of Coen Jansen's customers. In fact I myself sent an exciting geranium to Coen a few years ago. It was a *G. phaeum* that a couple visiting one of our Open Garden events had brought with them from their own garden (see page 101). This plant will now be available to buy as *G. phaeum* 'Conny Broe'.

Above: From Kazakhstan comes the parent plant of this wonderful blue geranium, which we can now look forward to. It will soon be available for sale.

Next year, once it has been published in Coen Janson's catalogue, it will be registered in the international list of geraniums, the *Checklist of Geranium Cultivar Names.*

It was also a customer who was "responsible" for Coen's intense interest in geraniums. Many years ago, this customer brought him a *G. psilostemon*, and Coen was so taken by the attractive flowers that he was converted on the spot. Now Coen Jansen is famous both for his large selection of geraniums at the nursery and for his own introductions, which include:

   G. 'Chocolate Candy'
   G. clarkei 'Kashmir Green'

   G. 'Madelon'
   G. ×oxonianum 'Ankum's White'
   G. phaeum 'Golden Samobor'
   G. phaeum 'Lisa'
   G. sanguineum 'Ankum's Pride'
   G. sylvaticum 'Ice Blue'
   G. sylvaticum 'Immaculée'
   G.. sylvaticum 'Lilac Time'

Right: Coen Jansen demonstrates how high, or rather, how low this new blue geranium from Kazakhstan will eventually grow.

1 *G.* 'Lakwijk Star', which will soon be on sale, has very attractive, large dark leaves and brilliant magenta flowers. 2 A look into one of the covered areas, where many geraniums grow until they are large enough for sale. 3 Coen Jansen with a group of *G. phaeum* 'Margaret Wilson'. 4 *G. maculatum* 'Elizabeth Ann', from America, is one of the newest geraniums on the market. 5 *G.* 'Lakwijk Star' has large, green and purple leaves.

New varieties in the pipeline

When we visited Coen Jansen, we naturally also wanted to check if he had any new varieties in the pipeline, and of course he had. There were several geraniums worth waiting for growing in the garden at the nursery. Among them was a new *G. wlassovianum*, for example, with very large magenta flowers and particularly attractive, very dark green leaves with purple edges.

This plant is probably the result of some geranium or other being crossed with *G. wlassovianum*, although nobody knows exactly which species. It is extremely seldom that *G. wlassovianum* crosses with anything.

(The only named hybrid is *G.* 'Khan', where *G. sanguineum* has crossed with *G. wlassovianum*.) This new *G. wlassovianum* hybrid has been discovered by a customer and will now be called *G.* 'Lakwijk Star'.

For a long time, many of us have yearned for a blue cranesbill that is not too tall, and now we've got one. It is one of Coen's seedlings, and it looks very promising. The plant originates from a group of seeds that Coen was given. The seeds were from an unknown geranium in Kazakhstan. The plant, which is illustrated on page 41, has not yet been given a name.

Another new blue cranesbill in the pipeline is a *G. platyanthum* (synonym *G. eriostemon*), a seedling with flowers of a completely unbelievable blue colour, which has been discovered by another of the nursery's customers; the usual flower colour of *G. platyanthum* is a rather dull bluish purple.

On a walk around the garden, we pass other geraniums. "Here is a new one from America. It is a *G. maculatum* with completely dark brown leaves. It's called 'Elizabeth Ann'," explains Coen, and then leads us to *G.* 'Jolly Bee'. His nursery was one of the very few permitted to sell a batch of this geranium. Coen talks enthusiastically about the plant, and 'Jolly Bee' is certainly extremely beautiful—large pure blue flowers

with a chalk white centre, dark veins and black stamens, somewhat similar to a particularly lush *G. wlassovianum* 'Buxton's Blue'. *Geranium* 'Jolly Bee', which is indeed a hybrid of *G. wlassovianum*, comes from Marco Noort, in Warmond, Holland. This plant is patented, in other words you may not propagate it for sale without paying a fee, although you are allowed to do so for your own garden. "Now I no longer want to propagate 'Buxton's Blue'", says Coen. "This is much, much better. It flowers much earlier and longer; it begins to flower as early as the end of May. The plant also has larger flowers and is particularly vigorous."

Not far from *G.* 'Jolly Bee' stands a shiny "red" 'Buxton's Blue' that makes me forget that I almost felt a bit sorry for the old Buxton! I have to know what it is. "It's called *G. wlassovianum* 'Roze Tinten'," says Coen, explaining that in the pastures of Nepal, *G. wlassovianum* can be found in all possible colours: white, pink, red, purple and blue, with and without veins— 'Buxton's Blue' is only one of the many varieties. This one, 'Roze Tinten', grows more strongly and is more vigorous than 'Buxton's Blue'.

As around 40 percent of the nursery's stock is taken up with new introductions, there is always something new and exciting

to look at. Coen is blessed with a burning curiosity to know what is going on in the plant world, and travels every year to visit friends among his colleagues in the United Kingdom to find out what is new, but news also reaches him from good colleagues in the U.S.A., Germany and elsewhere in Holland.

We have a chat about plants in general and geraniums in particular. I ask what he looks for in a new geranium, and Coen replies that the plant must naturally be different from other varieties, better and healthy, of course, and adds, "The most important thing: it must appeal to me. I must go wild about it!" The road to success, Coen believes, is being able to choose, or rather, to discard.

Coen has an eye for a good new plant and can spot what is appealing and different, and he does not worry about discarding plants. Coen has succeeded in creating a successful, well-known nursery with a stable clientele. Whether this is due to a growing interest in specialist nurseries is difficult to tell, but the main reason, in any case, is clear—customers here meet a very knowledgeable and enthusiastic nurseryman. (For Coen Jansen's details, see Address List.)

Far left: *G. sylvaticum* 'Lilac Time'
Left: *G.* 'Joy'
Below: Many of the geraniums in my garden form light clouds of white, pink and blue flowers.

Alphabetical List of Species and Hybrids

The geraniums described on the following pages are arranged alphabetically with key facts listed.

There is information about the height; whether the species or hybrid requires sun or shade; the colour and diameter of the flower (if I know this); the flowering season; the propagation method, whether by seed, rhizomes, division, basal cuttings, root cuttings or stem cuttings. (Please refer to the "Propagating Hardy Geraniums" on pages 35–39 for more details on the various methods.)

The heights given are naturally only approximate, as there are many factors that affect this including the soil type and locality. Where a height range is specified, such as 30–60 cm, this means that the smallest variety is approximately 30 cm and the largest is about 60 cm.

In the same way, the flower colour may be specified, for example as white, pink or cyclamen, but all depending on how the colours of the varieties vary.

The plates show the flower heads at their actual size, which can vary somewhat according to the soil type and the age of the plant. The soil may also affect the shade of the flower colour.

The leaves are, for obvious reasons, not shown at their actual size on the plates, although they are all in correct proportion.

It is difficult to specify the season and flowering period precisely, as not all years are the same. At the time of writing, on 22 April, the first *G. sanguineum* has appeared, due to the extremely warm weather we experienced at Easter this year. I have never seen this before. It is normally only towards the beginning of June that this species

begins to flower. I have opted to describe the seasons as:

Early summer (as a rule from the end of May to the beginning of July).

Midsummer (as a rule from the middle of June to the middle of August).

All summer (as a rule from June to late in the autumn).

Late summer (as a rule from the end of July into September).

The climate of Denmark is equivalent to United States Department of Agriculture (U.S.D.A.) hardiness zone 5, almost 6.

An "×" between two geraniums in the list designates the parentage of a hybrid.

After the main entry, there is a section "Other" for the species and hybrids for which there is something of particular note to record. You might like to read this during the long dark winter evenings.

G. asphodeloides 'Prince Regent'

Descriptions of Species and Hybrids

Geranium albanum

Height: 30–45 cm
Position: Sun, partial shade
Flower: Warm pink with magenta
               veins. 2.5 cm
Season: Midsummer
Propagation: Division, seed

Geranium albanum originates from the southeastern Caucasus and the neighbouring part of Iran.

The species has large, round, indented leaves. The indentations extend approximately halfway down the middle of the leaf. Unfortunately, the attractive pink flowers sit on long, thin stems, so the plant tends to sprawl. One possible way to overcome this is to place it by shrubs which the plant can then climb up.

Although it seems hard to believe, the species name refers to the Caucasus. An area that is now known as Daghestan has the Latin name "Albania". It was actually part of the Roman Empire.

Geranium albiflorum

Height: 30–45 cm
Position: Partial shade
Flower: White with purple veins. 1 cm
Season: Early summer and often again
               later
Propagation: Division, seed

Geranium albiflorum grows wild in central Asia and northeastern Russia. The species name refers to the white flowers. These very attractive, funnel-shaped flowers are, unfortunately, small and few. Therefore, most people will probably not want to place this species in the best bed in their garden, but in more naturalistic plantings. *Geranium albiflorum* has leaves reminiscent of *G. sylvaticum*. The stems and sepals are an attractive reddish colour. The edge of the leaves is the same red-brown shade.

Geranium 'Ann Folkard'

(*G. procurrens* × *G. psilostemon*)
Height: 50 cm
Position: Sun, partial shade
Flower: Warm magenta-red with black
               eye. 4 cm
Season: Midsummer
Propagation: Division, stem cuttings,
               no seeds

G. 'Ann Folkard'

Geranium 'Ann Folkard' is a hybrid that displays characteristics of both its parents. From *G. procurrens* the hybrid gets its long stems and from *G. psilostemon* its "shocking" magenta-red flower and black eye. *Geranium* 'Ann Folkard' was found in the garden of Oliver Folkard in Lincolnshire, England, in 1973. The leaves and flowers of *G.* 'Ann Folkard' provide a particularly lively colour combination. With its yellowish green foliage it brings a lush element to any border. The only negative thing about the plant is that one of the parents, *G. procurrens*, is not hardy in my experience, which means that *G.* 'Ann Folkard' may not come through very cold, wet winters, when you would be advised to cover it and keep your fingers crossed.

See the plate with *G. psilostemon* and hybrids on page 107.

Geranium 'Anne Thomson'

(*G. procurrens* × *G. psilostemon*)
Height: 50 cm
Position: Sun, partial shade
Flower: Warm magenta-red with black
               eye
Season: Midsummer
Propagation: Division, stem cuttings,
               no seed

Geranium 'Anne Thomson' is a hybrid with the same parents as *G.* 'Ann Folkard'. These two "sisters" are very similar to each other. 'Anne Thomson' differs from 'Ann Folkard' in having slightly smaller flowers, the foliage is less yellowish green in colour, and finally 'Anne Thomson' is slightly more compact than 'Ann Folkard'. Unfortunately, 'Anne Thomson', like 'Ann Folkard', is not reliably hardy and may suffer in a very cold wet winter.

See the plate with *G. psilostemon* and hybrids on page 107.

Geranium ×antipodeum

(*G. sessiliflorum* × *G. traversii*)
See page 130.

Geranium argenteum

See page 52.

Geranium aristatum

Height: 50 cm
Position: Sun, partial shade
Flower: Pale mauve with bold veins.
               2.5 cm
Season: Midsummer
Propagation: Division, seed

Geranium aristatum originates in the mountainous areas of Albania, the former Yugoslavia and northwestern Greece. It is closely related to *G. phaeum*, and both the flowers and leaves are similar to that species.

Geranium aristatum also has reflexed petals, but the flowers are unmistakable due to the stripes on the petals. For one reason or another this species often has three flowers together instead of the usual two.

However, *G. aristatum* differs in other ways from *G. phaeum*—its seeds are difficult to germinate (whereas *G. phaeum* seeds with abandon) and it dies down over winter.

Cut down *G. aristatum* when it is starting to look tired. The plant will then form healthy new leaves and flowers.

Geranium asphodeloides

Height:	45 cm
Position:	Sun, partial shade
Flower:	White, pink, or lilac with stripes. 2.5 cm
Season:	Early summer and midsummer
Propagation:	Division, seed (but the varieties are not true to type)

Geranium asphodeloides is an incredibly easy plant to grow. It is available in three subspecies:

Geranium asphodeloides subsp. *asphodeloides*, which comes from southern Europe. The star-shaped flowers are white, pink or dark pink with dark veins.

Geranium asphodeloides subsp. *crenophilum* is from Lebanon and Syria. The flowers are dark pink with dark veins.

Geranium asphodeloides subsp. *sintenisii* comes from northern Turkey. The plant is hairy and the hairs are red at the top. The flowers are light pink or dark purple.

Although the species' flowers are small, you can easily see them as there are so many of them: the plant looks like a small, light cloud of flowers. Flowering starts early, so the plant may benefit from being cut down after midsummer, when it seems a little tired after its first major flowering. It will soon return in full force.

Use as ground cover under trees that do not cast very deep shade. This geranium,

which can tolerate dryness, is particularly suitable for rock gardens or drystone walls. In beds, it can weave itself in among other plants and adorn those that are past their best, as well as hiding the unattractive stems of roses. The plant seeds itself a fair amount, so you should make sure it is cut down in time, unless you want it to cover a wild area or a more informal part of the garden.

When you sow seeds from this species, you can count on getting *G. asphodeloides*. A sterile hybrid has only been found once (in 1912), of which one parent was *G. asphodeloides* and the other *G. bohemicum*.

Varieties

'Prince Regent'
Lilac-coloured flowers with dark stripes. It starts flowering very early. Introduced in 1990.

'Starlight'
Completely white flowers with wider petals than 'Prince Regent'. 'Starlight' is a cross between the subspecies from southern Europe and the one from Lebanon and Syria. As a result, I have noticed that it is not quite as hardy as 'Prince Regent'. The plant originated in 1980 in the geranium bed in University Botanic Garden, Cambridge, England. Introduced in 1990.

Geranium 'Bertie Crûg'

(*G. endressii* × *G. papuanum*)

Height:	5 cm
Position:	Sun
Flower:	Deep pink
Season:	Midsummer, perhaps longer
Propagation:	Stem cuttings

Geranium 'Bertie Crûg' is, unfortunately, not as tough as its namesake, the little terrier at the Welsh nursery Crûg Farm, after which it is named. The hybrid, which is a seedling found at the nursery, is simply not strong and hardy. This is because one of

the plant's parents, *G. papuanum*, originates from tropical areas. *Geranium* 'Bertie Crûg' is a rock garden plant, as it needs very well drained soil. It has small, shiny, bronze-coloured leaves and creeping growth. The small flowers appear over a long period. Although not hardy or long-lived in the United Kingdom, it is very popular there. I have therefore included it in my book—also I can't resist the fact that it was named after a dog.

Geranium papuanum originates from the mountains in Papua New Guinea. It is a small, creeping plant with shiny, dark green and deeply indented leaves. It looks like a mini *G. sanguineum*. The flowers are single, as they are in *G. sanguineum*. *Geranium papuanum* has small, bright pink flowers, 2.5 cm across, with dark veins. The species easily puts down roots from its stems.

The Alpine Garden Society Bulletin, edition 56 (1988), has details of the introduction of the species as well as a picture (see Bibliography).

G. 'Blue Cloud'

Geranium 'Blue Cloud'

Height:	35 cm
Position:	Sun, partial shade
Flower:	Completely light bluish purple, star-shaped with veins. 4 cm
Season:	Midsummer
Propagation:	Division

Left: I hope this annual *G. bohemicum* will sow itself in suitable quantities in my rock garden, as it is a very appealing shade of blue.

Geranium 'Blue Cloud' is a seedling, probably from *G.* 'Nimbus'. It has very attractive, quite fine leaves. The plant grows slowly, and its stems grow outwards.

Use in beds or under a specimen shrub. Under shrubs there is not much room above, but plenty to the sides, which is perfect for the habit of 'Blue Cloud'.

Geranium 'Blue Sunrise'

(*G.* 'Ann Folkard' × *G. wallichianum* 'Buxton's Variety')

Height: 35 cm
Position: Sun
Flower: Reddish purple. 3 cm
Season: Midsummer
Propagation: Division, difficult. Stem cuttings possibly

Geranium 'Blue Sunrise' originated in Holland at the nursery of Hans Kramer (Kwerkerij De Hessenhof) in 1992. The most interesting thing about the plant is its yellow-green leaves. The flowers in themselves are not very special, but the yellow foliage gives them a warm magenta tone. Hans Kramer has explained that the seedling was found close to *G. wallichianum* 'Buxton's Variety' and *G.* 'Ann Folkard', so it is assumed that these are the parents, not least because it has characteristics of both. But you can never be sure. Originally the plant was called *G.* 'Verguld Saffier', but when Blooms of Bressingham nursery took over the plant for patenting and sale the name was changed in 1999.

Geranium bohemicum

Height: 30–50 cm
Position: Sun
Flower: Lavender with dark veins. 1.5 cm
Season: Midsummer
Propagation: Seed

Geranium bohemicum is an annual or biennial that grows wild in eastern and central Europe. It occurs sporadically and is associated with areas scorched by fire. The species is a hairy plant that is suitable for rock gardens or landscape gardens. Its attractive flowers, however, make the trouble of sowing it regularly worthwhile.

G. 'Brookside'

Geranium 'Brookside'

(*G. pratense* × *G. clarkei* 'Kashmir Purple')

Height: 70 cm
Position: Sun or partial shade
Flower: Blue with white centre. 4 cm
Season: Midsummer
Propagation: Division. There may be seeds, but this variety is not true to seed

Geranium 'Brookside' appeared as a seedling in 1970 in the University Botanic Garden, Cambridge.

The leaves are finely indented, and the flower is a much purer blue than, for instance, the flowers of *G. himalayense*, which has a little red mixed in with the blue. The plant stands as a large, blue cloud for a very long period. Use in beds, perhaps together with white-flowered perennials, which will nicely match the white centre of *G.* 'Brookside'. Plants went on sale in 1989.

G. 'Blue Sunrise'

Geranium ×cantabrigiense

Geranium ×cantabrigiense

Height:	25 cm
Position:	Sun or shade
Flower:	White, pale pink, pure pink or purplish red. 2.5 cm
Season:	Early summer
Propagation:	Division, rhizomes (sterile, no seed)

Geranium ×cantabrigiense is a cross between *G. macrorrhizum* and *G. dalmaticum*, a hybrid that can occur in nature. However, most varieties are produced by intentional crossing work. These hybrids are sterile (so do not sow themselves) and form excellent ground cover. They can also be placed in a rock garden or at the front of a bed.

The foliage, which smells pleasant, has a wonderful colour in the autumn, and the plant is practically evergreen. The leaves and stems are shiny and hairless, which means that *G. ×cantabrigiense* can generally be distinguished from *G. macrorrhizum*, whose varieties are almost never hairless.

Geranium ×cantabrigiense can grow virtually anywhere, and as this hybrid is more compact than macrorrhizum geraniums, varieties can easily be controlled if space is short.

G. ×cantabrigiense 'Berggarten' G. ×cantabrigiense 'Biokovo' G. ×cantabrigiense 'Cambridge'

G. ×cantabrigiense 'Harz' G. ×cantabrigiense 'Karmina' G. ×cantabrigiense 'Lohfelden'

G. ×cantabrigiense 'Rosalina' G. ×cantabrigiense 'St. Ola'

Varieties

G. ×cantabrigiense '**Berggarten**'
Brilliant pink.

G. ×cantabrigiense '**Biokovo**'
Pale pink with deep pink veins. Attractive, but not as dense a plant as, for example, 'Cambridge'.

G. ×cantabrigiense '**Cambridge**'
Purplish red. Vigorous. Indistinguishable from 'Karmina'.

G. ×cantabrigiense '**Harz**'
Almost white.

G. ×cantabrigiense '**Karmina**'
Purplish red. Indistinguishable from 'Cambridge'.

G. ×cantabrigiense '**Lohfelden**'
Delicate pink. Large flowers. From Heinz Klose's nursery in Lohfelden, Germany.

G. ×cantabrigiense '**Rosalina**'
Mauve. Selected seedling from the Sarastro nursery in Austria.

G. ×cantabrigiense '**St. Ola**'
Pure white. Alan Bremner crossed *G. macrorrhizum* 'Album' and *G. dalmaticum* 'Album', thereby creating this variety. Introduced in 1994 (see page 33).

Other

In 1974, botanists at the University of Cambridge started hybridizing experiments between *G. macrorrhizum* and *G. dalmaticum*. Plants were cross pollinated. With *G. dalmaticum* as the "mother", three seeds were produced, but none of these were viable. Using *G. macrorrhizum* as the "mother", five seeds developed, one of which sprouted and became the plant we know as *G. ×cantabrigiense* 'Cambridge'.

In 1977, Dr. Hans Simon found a hybrid of *G. macrorrhizum* and *G. dalmaticum* growing near the town of Makarska in the Biokovo mountains in southern Dalmatia. Strangely enough, neither of these two species was growing in the vicinity. Simon named the plant after the place where it was found and put it into production at his Gärtnerei "Simon" nursery in Marktheidenfeld in Germany.

The name *G. ×cantabrigiense* was given to the hybrids by Peter Yeo in 1985.

G. cataractarum

Geranium cataractarum

Height: 15 cm
Position: Sun, partial shade
Flower: Warm pink with brilliant orange stamens. 2 cm
Season: Midsummer
Propagation: Seed

Geranium cataractarum comes from southern Spain and Morocco. The leaves, which are small and indented, are aromatic. The main attraction of the plant is its orange-red stamens. If *G. cataractarum* is left dry, it will generally survive the winter. It is thus best suited to a rock garden. It is a short-lived plant, but readily sows itself.

Geranium 'Chantilly'

(*G. gracile* × *G. renardii*)
See page 112.

G. 'Chantilly'

Geranium 'Chocolate Candy'

See under G. 'Kahlua', page 68.

Above: *G. ×cantabrigiense* 'St. Ola' and *G. himalayense*.
Below: *G. ×cantabrigiense* 'Biokovo' and 'Karmina' photographed in a private garden. For years, they have stood next to the entrance at the gable end of the house where they have adapted to a windy location.

G. 'Ballerina'

G. 'Carol'

G. 'Laurence Flatman'

G. 'Purple Pillow'

G. subcaulescens 'Giuseppii'

G. subcaulescens 'Purpureum'

G. subcaulescens 'Splendens'

G. ×lindavicum 'Apple Blossom'

Geranium cinereum Group

Height:	10–15 cm
Position:	Sun
Flower:	White, pink, magenta, many with black eye, many with veins. 3–4 cm
Season:	Early summer, some varieties a little longer
Propagation:	Division, basal cuttings, root cuttings, seed (the varieties are not true to seed)

The classification, or division, of the best geraniums for rock gardens has just been changed (Aedo, 1996; Yeo, 2001). Several geraniums that were previously subspecies have now been raised to a species—which is lucky, because the name *G. cinereum* subspecies *subcaulescens* varietas *subcaulescens* is almost enough to make you feel ill. *Geranium subcaulescens* is all you need now. Geraniums in the Cinereum Group have attractive, indented leaves, often in silver-grey shades, and the flowers are large in relation to the small, compact plants. Some of the group's members are very difficult to grow. For details about cultivation, see "Hardy Geraniums for Rock Gardens" (page 20).

Geraniums in this group cannot easily be mass-produced at home in the garden, but they can be propagated with a little patience. Various methods of taking cuttings are shown on pages 37 and 38. Naturally, you can also sow seed of these geraniums, but this is somewhat academic, as 'Ballerina', for example, does not produce many seeds. There are hardly any, and seeds from the other members of the Cinereum Group can, I understand, only be acquired from specialist societies (see Address List).

The nursery industry propagates varieties such as 'Ballerina' using meristem culture (see page 13). We ordinary gardeners cannot manage that, but then on the other hand we don't need several thousand plants at the same time.

The Cinereum Group

The following geraniums are included in this group:

Geranium argenteum
Leaves are round and very indented. White to pink flowers. The species originates from Italy, the former Yugoslavia and the Alpine areas of France. Difficult to grow.

Geranium cinereum
This comes from the Pyrénées and has pale pink flowers (4 cm), with mauve veins. This is one of the group members with the most deeply indented leaves.

Cinereum varieties include:
'Album', which has pure white flowers and is difficult to grow.

G. ×lindavicum
(*G. argenteum* × *G. subcaulescens*)
A hybrid that originated in gardens. The varieties are difficult to grow.

Varieties include:
'Apple Blossom', which is delicate pink with thin, dark red veins; the leaves have a silver sheen. From Alan Bloom of Bressingham.
'Lissadell' has magenta flowers with clear veins.

G. makmelicum

Previously known as *G. cinereum* var. *obtusilobum*, this has very small, light green leaves. The flowers are pale pink and attractively veined. Very seldom commercially available.

G. subcaulescens

This grows wild in the Balkans and in northeastern Turkey. The varieties produce some of the most eye-catching flower colours within the *Geranium* genus— colours that are not easy to describe, much less photograph. It is almost as if the camera refuses to believe its eye. If you think about dog roses (*Rosa rugosa*), you know the colour scale we are talking about.

The following varieties of *G. subcaulescens* are the easiest to grow within the Cinereum Group.

'Giuseppii' is dark magenta-red with a dark centre. The variety is named after a plant collector, Dr. Paul Giuseppi, who was president of the Alpine Garden Society (see the Address List).

'Giuseppina' is dark carmine red with a black eye. It is lower-growing than 'Giuseppii'.

'Glühwein' has wine red flowers with a black eye.

'Purpureum' was kind enough to bloom again as I was writing this section (August 2003), and I fetched a petal from a dog rose for comparison. 'Purpureum' is a touch more blue. Besides its bold magenta colour, this brilliant flower is also blessed with black veins and a black eye. Created in 1937 by Georg Arends.

'Signal' has brilliant carmine red flowers that appear over a very long period.

'Splendens' has flowers that are brilliant dark pink with a black eye (Georg Arends, 1930).

Hybrids

These hybrids, like the *G. subcaulescens* varieties, are not so difficult to grow.
'Ballerina' (*G. cinereum* × *G. subcaulescens*).

The base colour of the petals is pale lilac and they have bold dark purple veins. Very dark centre. From 1962, Alan Bloom, Bressingham.

'Carol' has a very attractive deep pink colour. The flowers have dark veins and a dark centre.

'Laurence Flatman' from 1980 has the same parents as 'Ballerina' and also comes from

Alan Bloom. This variety is similar to 'Ballerina', but the flowers are slightly darker, more of a burgundy, and appear in more intense colours.

'Purple Pillow' has very dark flowers with black-red veins and a dark centre. The colour is halfway between blood red and burgundy.

Geranium clarkei

G. clarkei
'Kashmir Green'

G. clarkei
'Kashmir Pink'

G. clarkei
'Kashmir Purple'

G. clarkei
'Kashmir White'

Geranium clarkei

Height:	40 cm
Position:	Sun
Flower:	White with veins (green or purple), bluish purple, delicate pink. 4–5 cm
Season:	Early summer
Propagation:	Rhizomes, some varieties from seed

Geranium clarkei originates from Kashmir. The leaf is deeply indented, the petals are like filigree work and the flowers sit on thin stems. *Geranium clarkei* has rhizomes, by which it spreads. The variety 'Kashmir Purple' grows particularly profusely and is probably too aggressive for small gardens. If you want ground cover for a large rose bed, and you don't mind the plant taking up all the space, then it is a good choice. The three other varieties, which grow less strongly, can easily be put in a bed with other perennials.

Varieties

G. clarkei 'Kashmir Green'
White with green veins. Introduced by Coen Jansen.

G. clarkei 'Kashmir Pink'
Pink. The large flowers look as if they are made of tissue paper. The variety is a seedling from 'Kashmir Purple'. It originated in Blackthorn Nursery, England and was introduced in 1990.

G. clarkei 'Kashmir Purple'
Bluish purple with red veins. Quickly runs away with its underground stems. Virtually true from seed.

G. clarkei 'Kashmir White'
White with magenta veins, which give the flower a slightly grey sheen. Partially true from seed; some seedlings are like 'Kashmir Purple'.

Other

Peter Yeo named the species in 1985. He chose to name this geranium after C. B. Clarke (1832–1906), who was the supervisor of the botanical garden in Calcutta. Clarke actually collected the earliest known example of the species, which is in the herbarium at the Royal Botanic Gardens, Kew, England.

Geranium clarkei was originally regarded as a form of *G. pratense*, which is why you still see the names *G. pratense* 'Kashmir Purple' and *G. pratense* 'Kashmir White'.

Geranium clarkei has been crossed with *G. collinum* and with *G. pratense*. This has

Left: *G. clarkei* 'Kashmir Pink' is a seedling from *G. clarkei* 'Kashmir Purple', which is generally considered to come true from seed.

G. collinum

The highly indented leaves, when they appear in the spring, are often variegated with creamy yellow and pink mixed in with the green. *Geranium collinum* tolerates drought well, but unfortunately it has a loose growth form, which makes it best suited for wild gardens. *Geranium collinum* is one of the parents of *G.* 'Nimbus' (*G. collinum* × *G. clarkei*).

given us two really good garden plants, *G.* 'Nimbus' and *G.* 'Brookside' respectively, both originating in the experimental beds in the botanical garden belonging to the University of Cambridge, England. *Geranium* 'Kashmir Blue' is a hybrid (*G. pratense albiflorum* × *G. clarkei* 'Kashmir White'). The Belgian Ivan Louette (see page 66) crossed the two species some time in the mid-1980s. The variety is virtually identical to a light blue *G. pratense*.

Below: *G. clarkei* 'Kashmir Green' was introduced by Coen Jansen.

Geranium collinum

Height:	60 cm
Position:	Sun
Flower:	Violet-pink. 3 cm
Season:	Midsummer
Propagation:	Division, seed

Geranium collinum grows wild in a large area from southeastern Europe and eastern Turkey across Central Asia to Siberia and the Himalayas. The species name means "growing on hills". (Some of the hills are quite high!) As the species grows over such enormous areas, it displays variation. Some have pale pink flowers, while others have dark pink ones, and yet others have red veins on their petals.

Geranium 'Cyril's Fancy'

(*G. albiflorum* × *G. sylvaticum*)

Height:	75 cm
Position:	Partial shade, sun
Flower:	Pale magenta
Season:	Early summer
Propagation:	Division

Geranium 'Cyril's Fancy' is a hybrid discovered by Cyril Foster, a gardener in northern England, and introduced by Catforth Gardens in 1997. This hybrid makes a large, upright plant similar to *G. sylvaticum*. It has large, star-shaped flowers, which appear in huge quantities.

Geranium dalmaticum

Height:	10–15 cm
Position:	Sun, partial shade
Flower:	White, pink. 2.5 cm
Season:	Early summer
Propagation:	Division, rhizomes, seed (but almost none set)

Geranium dalmaticum grows wild along the Dalmatian coast of Croatia. This plant's small size makes it excellent for a rock garden, but if you don't have one, it can be placed at the edge of a bed where it will not be overrun by other plants. *Geranium dalmaticum* is extremely easy to deal with. It soon forms an excellent, close ground cover. The flowers are of the same type as

G. macrorrhizum. Old plants refuse to flower, but they can easily be revitalized. Split the plant up, throw away the oldest part in the middle, and plant the outer parts in fresh soil. The indented, rounded and completely smooth leaves will be attractively coloured in the autumn.

The plant was introduced for garden use in 1947 by Walter Ingwersen (see page 73). There is a white form of *G. dalmaticum*, known as 'Album', which was introduced in 1956. It seems that this prefers a little more shade, but I find difficult to get it to come to anything. *Geranium dalmaticum* is one of the parents of *G. ×cantabrigiense*.

Geranium 'Dilys'

(*G. procurrens* × *G. sanguineum*)

Height:	20 cm
Position:	Sun
Flower:	Magenta with dark eye and dark veins. 3 cm
Season:	Midsummer
Propagation:	Division

Geranium 'Dilys' is one of the few hybrids in which *G. sanguineum* is involved. Alan Bremner (see page 33) succeeded in crossing *G. sanguineum* with *G. procurrens*. As with other crosses using *G. sanguineum*, *G.* 'Dilys' most resembles *G. sanguineum* (see page 118 for more details). The plant is named after Dilys Davies, a prominent member of the Hardy Plant Society in the United Kingdom (see Address List).

Geranium 'Dilys' may not be reliably hardy, as *G. procurrens* is one of its parents. However, it is one of the plants I want to try, as it flowers from August until the frost comes.

Left: Many *G. endressii* and *G. ×oxonianum* form close mounds of flowers. Here, *G. endressii* 'Betty Catchpole' can be seen in the foreground.

Geranium donianum

Height:	30–40 cm
Position:	Sun
Flower:	Deep pink
Season:	Midsummer
Propagation:	Seed

Geranium donianum originates from the Himalayas, Tibet and China and is named after a British botanist, D. Don. The species has kidney-shaped leaves that are very deeply indented and marbled in shades of green. The Swedish gardening magazine *Trädgårdsamatören*, no. 1 (1998), contains a fine picture of *G. donianum* in an article, "Geraniums for mountain gardens", by the Norwegian Ole P. Olsen, who enthuses about the plants, which originate from seeds he has sown; *Geranium donianum* produces more flowers than any other geranium he has ever had. He writes that the seedlings were put in a well-drained mixture of sand and topsoil with spruce needles added. *Geranium donianum* does not appear until late in the spring, so it is important to be patient and not dig in the area, writes Olsen. In the first year, the plant only puts out a few leaves, but the next year it puts out full flowers and leaves. In the autumn, the plant produces many seeds which easily sprout. In conclusion, Ole P. Olsen writes about *G. donianum*: "It has seldom been cultivated and the English have had problems getting it established. Here in northern Norway, it is fully hardy."

I too had read that the English had problems with this species in *The Gardener's Guide to Growing Hardy Geraniums* (1994) by Bath and Jones, where, with reference to *G. donianum*, one of the authors states that: "in my experience it is not long-lived, but would make an attractive addition to the rock garden if one could discover the formula for longevity."

G. endressii
'Betty Catchpole'

Geranium endressii

Height:	45 cm
Position:	Sun, partial shade
Flower:	Pink, 3 cm
Season:	Entire summer
Propagation:	Rhizomes, seed (but crosses easily arise)

Geranium endressii grows wild in southwestern Europe. It has long rhizomes just below the surface of the ground.

The flowers are funnel-shaped and have the odd feature of becoming darker with age; they fade in reverse. You seldom see this species planted in gardens, but its progeny, the hybrids formed when it has been crossed with *G. versicolor*, are used.

A popular geranium, and one of the most common garden plants here in Denmark, is often sold under the name *G. endressii* 'Rose Clair'. This plant is actually *G. ×oxonianum* 'Rose Clair'. It can be hard to tell if a variety belongs to *G. endressii* or is a *G. ×oxonianum*. Another example is the plant sold under the names of *G. endressii* 'Beholder's Eye' and *G. ×oxonianum* 'Beholder's Eye'. In the same way, 'Wargrave Pink' and 'Betty Catchpole' appear under both designations.

G. endressii
'Beholder's Eye'

Left: With *G. erianthum*, the varieties with light-coloured flowers grow slowly, so the variety 'Calm Sea', pictured, does not grow especially fast.

Geranium erianthum

Height: 45–60 cm
Position: Sun, partial shade
Flower: White, bluish purple or pale
               violet, often with dark veins.
               3.5 cm
Season: Early summer
Propagation: Division, seed (varieties are
               not true to seed)

Geranium erianthum grows wild in eastern Siberia, Japan, Alaska and Canada. This is a huge area, and the species is therefore variable. Its height ranges from 45 to 60 cm, and the flowers may be white, bluish purple or pale violet. The flowers often have dark veins. The leaves are deeply indented, divided into 7 or 9 lobes which overlap completely. Joy Jones and Trevor Bath write in their book *Hardy Geraniums* (1994) that this is one of those plants that has a quiet beauty and is always suitable. They say that the varieties are particularly attractive grown together with blue-leaved hostas.

   Geranium erianthum flowers very early and for several weeks. Later in the season, it often flowers again. The leaves take on attractive colours in the autumn.

Varieties

G. erianthum 'Calm Sea'
60 cm. Pale violet with dark veins. This plant came to the University Botanic Garden, Cambridge, England, from the botanical garden in Vladivostok, Russia.
G. erianthum 'Neptune'
50 cm. Dark bluish purple flowers without veins. The variety was named by David Hibberd, British author and former nurseryman. The University Botanic Garden, Cambridge, received this plant from the University of Uppsala, Sweden, which in turn had received it from a botanical garden in Japan.
G. erianthum 'Undine'
Low-growing. Pure white.

Other

In *G. erianthum* the speed of growth is, for one reason or another, linked to the flower colour. Erianthum geraniums with pale violet flowers grow extremely slowly, while the types with darker, bluish purple flowers grow faster.

When varieties are to be propagated by division, it is therefore quicker to produce many plants of 'Neptune' than of 'Calm Sea'. It would be easier to get many plants of 'Calm Sea' if it grew true from seed, so then you could merely sow seeds you had collected from it.

The German nurseryman Rolf Offenthal tried, therefore, to develop a seed strain that would come true. He failed, but he chose an attractive seedling from among 'Calm Sea's "grandchildren" (described in the German garden magazine *Gartenpraxis* in December 1999). He hoped to be able to launch the plant, but unfortunately it inherited the slow growth mentioned above. Offenthal has therefore decided that the seedling will never be available for sale. This is disappointing, as the description of 'Blue Eyes', as the seedling was called, sounded promising: pale violet-blue with a very dark violet centre.

Geranium 'Eva'

(*G. pratense* × *G. psilostemon*)

Height:	70 cm
Position:	Sun
Flower:	Very dark bluish purple, black veins, black eye and pale yellow stamens
Season:	Midsummer
Propagation:	Division, basal cuttings

Geranium 'Eva' has very eye-catching flowers and you can see immediately that there has to be some *G. psilostemon* in "her". However, the other parent, *G. pratense*, keeps itself in the background, as the leaves of *G.* 'Eva' are also similar to those of *G. psilostemon*.

Below: *Geranium* 'Eva' has very dark purple flowers that contrast well with the complementary colours of *Anthemis tinctoria* 'Sauce Hollandaise', with which it is planted.

Geranium 'Eva' is a very pleasing plant for beds. You can emphasize the unusual dark flowers by planting it with perennials that have flowers in delicate pastel colours. I have allowed *G.* 'Eva' to weave its stems into *Anthemis tinctoria* 'Sauce Hollandaise', which has pale yellow daisy flowers.

Right: *Geranium gracile is* often described as a "big brother" to *G. nodosum.*

Geranium farreri

Height:	10–15 cm
Position:	Sun
Flower:	Delicate pink with blue-black stamens. 2.5 cm
Season:	Early summer
Propagation:	Seed, basal cuttings

Geranium farreri grows in western China. It takes its name from a famous plant hunter and author, Reginald Farrer, who discovered the species in 1914. *Geranium farreri* has red stems and its small, kidney-shaped and indented leaves are reddish at the edges and underneath.

The flowers are usually attractive, so it is annoying that the plant finds it so difficult to survive the winter. The winter wet is what kills it off. The species is among the alpine geraniums (see "Geraniums for Rock Gardens", page 20).

Other

If you are mad about climbing and love mountain plants, it must be ideal to be born in a mountainous area to wealthy parents interested in gardens. Reginald Farrer, who was born in 1880 at Ingleborough Hall in Clapham in the Pennines, in England, had just such luck, although that was pretty much the only luck he had. In his childhood, he was schooled at home, as he was born with a harelip and cleft palate, which made talking difficult. However, as an adult he was educated at the University of Oxford, England, after which he travelled to Japan. The impressions he formed there were recorded in *The Garden of Asia* (1904), Farrer's first book, later followed by *My Rock Garden* (1907) and a two-volume work, *The English Rock Garden* (1919), among others.

During Reginald Farrer's first plant collecting trip, to northwestern China (Gansu Province) between 1914 and 1916, he found, at a height of almost 4000 metres, the geranium that would later bear his name. Many plants were collected by Farrer and his travelling companion William Purdom, and sent home to Great Britain. Unfortunately, this was an extremely bad time. Due to the First World War, there were virtually no staff at Kew or the other botanical gardens, so there was no one to deal with the plants. As a result, many of them were lost. After the war, Farrer went east again in 1919, this time to Burma with Cox. The trip was fatal for Farrer, who was overcome by his exertions and died on 17 October 1920.

Farrer has been extremely important for the style of gardening known as rock gardening. At the beginning of the twentieth century, the most important thing was not the alpine plants themselves but the huge constructions built for them. Wealthy men imported whole sections of cliffs for their gardens, which their gardeners arranged into "mountains". Most flower shows at this time had two categories: one for people who employed gardeners and one for people who didn't.

Farrer changed this trend, so that it became the plants that were the most important aspect and not the costly constructions, which he considered ridiculous. He recommended that people use stones or materials found in their locality and incorporate them into the garden to create a rock garden. In that way everything became more natural-looking and indeed worked out cheaper. Farrer was therefore instrumental in making this form of gardening more easily attainable for ordinary gardeners.

Geranium gracile

Height:	70 cm
Position:	Shade, partial shade
Flower:	Mauve, dark stripes pointing to the base of the funnel-shaped flower. 2.5 cm
Season:	Midsummer, often longer
Propagation:	Division, rhizomes, basal cuttings, seed (the varieties are not true to seed, and the species may vary)

Geranium gracile originates from northeastern Turkey and the Caucasus. It grows in woodland, so it should be planted in a shady bed in your garden. It is a very elegant plant for a woodland area, and it flowers for a very long time. The roots are a tangled mass, a tight clump with thick rhizomes weaving in and out. The plant's stems come up in a neat clump, so this cranesbill forms an excellent little bush. The attractive light green leaves are reminiscent of those of *G. nodosum*, although *G. gracile* leaves are larger.

As the flowers of the two species are also very similar, *G. gracile* is often described as a

G. gracile

G. nodosum

"big brother" to *G. nodosum* (see illustrations above).

I myself have had *G. gracile* for many years. Some of the plants have been in the same place for years, and probably flowered in deep shade month after month. In my woodland bed they have been excellent neighbours to members of the genera *Hosta*, *Bergenia* and *Epimedium*. Of course I also have other geraniums that tolerate shade, such as the different varieties of *G. phaeum*.

Varieties

> *G. gracile* 'Blanche'
> Pale pink.
> *G. gracile* 'Blush'
> Mauve.

Other

The excellent "eye lashes" on the petals mark the entrance to the flower's vital parts: "This way, pollinating insects!" The lines are not equally fine on all seedlings, but you can select the plants with the most "mascara".

The fact that *G. gracile* and *G. nodosum* are similar to each other is an example of what biologists call convergent development: individuals that live in the same environment develop the same characteristics. (A whale, which is a mammal, needs to be fish-like to be able to survive in water.) *Geranium gracile* and *G. nodosum* live in exactly the same types of woodland, but in different parts of the world at a huge distance from each other; *G. nodosum* is actually from southern Europe.

Above: *Geranium gracile* 'Blush' stands under the beech trees and catches the morning sun.

Geranium gymnocaulon

Height:	30–45 cm
Position:	Sun, partial shade
Flower:	Purplish blue with dark veins. 3.5 cm
Season:	Midsummer
Propagation:	Division, but best from seed

Geranium gymnocaulon originates from northeastern Turkey and the southwestern Caucasus. The species is very similar to *G. ibericum*, but flowers later. The thick roots creep over the ground, and the plant invites division. However, I have read that the small plants produced by division easily die, so propagation using seeds is better. I received my *G. gymnocaulon* with the information that I should plant it in a rock garden, and just let it look after itself and self sow. That is what it has done for a number of years, or rather my original plant's descendants have, as *G. gymnocaulon* is not long lived.

The species can tolerate some shade, but flowers best in full sunshine. *Geranium gymnocaulon* does not need a rock garden; it can also be planted in an ordinary border.

Left: David Hibberd has told me that he found a large-flowered geranium with the designation "G. Blue" at the Ingwersen nursery in England. In consultation with Paul Ingwersen, he gave it the name *G. himalayense* 'Baby Blue'. Paul is unable to say where the plant came from, so its origin will probably remain a mystery.

Below: Freja is enjoying the morning sun in front of *G. himalayense* 'Irish Blue'.

Above left: The colour blue takes over alongside this house in early summer, when *G. himalayense* flowers.

Above right: *G. himalayense* 'Plenum' looks like a little bluish purple rose. In the background is foliage of *Astrantia major* 'Sunningdale Variegated'.

Geranium himalayense

Height: 25–45 cm
Position: Sun or partial shade
Flower: Blue-violet with a red sheen
            around the whitish centre.
            4–6 cm
Season: Early summer and again a
            little later in the summer
Propagation: Division, rhizomes, seed
            (varieties not true from seed)

Geranium himalayense comes, as the name suggests, from the Himalayas. The plant is also called *G. grandiflorum* and *G. meeboldii*. It is the geranium that has the largest flowers and a very easy plant to grow. Give it space, as its underground stems like to spread out. However, the plant does not spread enough to be invasive.

The various varieties all have blue or blue-violet flowers. The leaves change colour attractively in the autumn; in the winter they disappear. Early in the spring, the plant shoots up to stand like scattered tufts in delicate shades of red and green. When the finely indented leaves unfold, the plant forms a light green carpet. Flowering starts in early summer, often in late May, and continues until late in the summer in fits and starts. It is ideal at the front of a bed or as ground cover under shrubs that do not cast full shade. The plant is light and airy, like a little blue cloud, and I cannot think of anything it does not look good with.

Geranium himalayense and hybrids

G. himalayense 'Baby Blue'

G. himalayense 'Devil's Blue'

G. himalayense 'Gravetye'

G. himalayense 'Irish Blue'

G. himalayense 'Plenum'

G. 'Johnson's Blue'

Varieties

Height is only given for shorter varieties.
G. himalayense 'Baby Blue'
30 cm. Blue-violet, very large flowers (6 cm).
G. himalayense 'Devil's Blue'
Blue-violet. Very similar to 'Gravetye', but a little larger in the flower. Introduced in 1999 from Croftway Nursery.
G. himalayense 'Gravetye'
Blue-violet with a red zone in the middle. The best-known himalayense geranium. It takes its name from the location where the influential and temperamental Irish garden writer William Robinson lived. His book *The Wild Garden* (1870) started a revolution in European gardening.
G. himalayense 'Irish Blue'
Light blue with shades of violet. Large flowers with less pronounced red zone than the other himalayense geraniums. Found around 1947 in a park in Ireland by Graham Stuart Thomas.
G. himalayense 'Plenum'
(synonym 'Birch Double')
25 cm. Dark violet. The flower, which measures approximately 3 cm, looks like a small, blue rose. The plant does not grow as fast as the other varieties, which is a pity, as it is very charming. 'Plenum' likes to have a little more care than the other himalayense geraniums, so give it a little compost. When I moved 'Plenum' from the rock garden to the lightest part of a shady bed, where the ground was not as dry but had woodland characteristics, it livened up significantly.

The name 'Birch Double' refers to Ingwersen's Birch Farm Nursery, which launched the variety. For more information about the Ingwersen family see the section "Other", on page 73.

Other

The first *G. himalayense* in Europe came to England, to Miss Ellen Willmott's garden, around 1900 from Sikkim. Miss Willmott (whose name is also remembered in other plants such as *Potentilla nepalensis* 'Miss Willmott') was incredibly rich with an insatiable interest in gardening. She could buy whatever she wanted for her gardens, and she did. Many new plants from foreign parts that came to Europe late in the nineteenth century are associated with her name, as she sponsored plant expeditions.

When sowing *G. himalayense* seeds, you can count on getting a himalayense geranium, as it very seldom crosses with other plants.

However, it has crossed with *G. pratense*, which is the relation it has most in common with genetically. The cross is called

Left: *Geranium himalayense* is an excellent ground-cover plant. Here it is being used in a most beautiful way to cover the ground between blue irises.

Right: *G. ibericum* 'White Zigana' was found in the Zigana mountain pass in 1994 by Michael Baron, while he was on holiday in northeastern Turkey.

G. 'Johnson's Blue'. There have been experiments to make this trick of nature again. In 1975 Dr. Helen Kiefer at Cambridge succeeded in getting two seedlings from the *G. himalayense* 'Gravetye' and *G. pratense* cross. One, currently sold under the name 'Helen', is supposed to be darker than 'Johnson's Blue'.

In Dundee, Scotland, John Ross of the Charter House Nursery succeeded in crossing *G. pratense* f. *albiflorum* with *G. himalayense* 'Gravetye'. The result is on sale under the name *G.* 'Nunwood Purple'.

Geranium **Summer Skies** ('Gernic') is a cross between *G. himalayense* 'Plenum' and *G. pratense*. It has double lavender-blue flowers with a pink sheen, which appear earlier than the other double pratense geraniums. It grows slowly and requires good care. Another cross with *G. himalayense* we will be hearing more about is *G.* **Rozanne** ('Gerwat'). The other parent in this case is *G. wallichianum*.

Geranium ibericum

Height:	30–45 cm
Position:	Sun
Flower:	Dark violet, light blue, white. 4–5 cm
Season:	Early summer
Propagation:	Division, seed (I don't know if the varieties come true from seed)

Geranium ibericum comes from northeastern Turkey and the Caucasus. The species name originates from Iberia, which is the Latin name for Georgia, in the Caucasus. The plant is hairy and has large, lobate leaves. The species is divided into two subspecies, *ibericum* and *jubatum*. This has no practical significance for gardeners. Recently, a white *G. ibericum* has appeared. When a nursery offers a plant bearing the name *G. ibericum*, it is rarely an example of the pure species. As a rule, there is really a hybrid behind the name. This hybrid is

G. ×magnificum, which is a cross between *G. ibericum* and *G. platypetalum*.

Varieties

G. ibericum subsp. jubatum 'Vital'
45 cm. Dark violet. Comes from Gärtnerei Simon (Dr. Hans Simon). It is a variety that tolerates dryness particularly well, and is, as its name suggests, very vital. Also available for sale as *G. ×magnificum* 'Vital'.

G. ibericum subsp. jubatum 'White Zigana'
45 cm. White with dark purple veins. Among all the blue-flowering *G. ibericum* in the Zigana mountain pass, Michael Baron

G. ibericum subsp. *jubatum* 'Vital'

found one with white flowers when he was on holiday in northeastern Turkey in 1994.
G. ibericum 'Ushguli Grijs'
30 cm. Grey-blue with dark, purple veins. Found in the Caucasus by Hans Kramer (of the Dutch nursery Kwerkerij De Hessenhof), where the plant just shone with its large, grey-blue flowers.

Other

Geranium ibericum was brought to our gardens by Appollon Mussin-Puschkin, a Russian ambassador in London, and his friend Baron von Bieberstein, who in 1802 went to the Caucasus on a three-year plant expedition. The results of this trip, besides *G. ibericum*, include *Scabiosa caucasica*, *Nepeta mussinii* and many other excellent garden plants.

In an old but excellent book by Jason Hill, *The Contemplative Gardener* (1939), the author writes in the chapter "The Evening Garden" about the effect of twilight on the colour of flowers. Red is the first colour we become unable to see when the light fades. He therefore advises people who want to sit outside enjoying their garden on summer evenings not to fill it

with red pelargoniums or other plants with pure red flowers.

Once the red colour cuts out, it affects the compound colours such as purple and violet, which are, of course, blue with red in. Blue-violet flowers will appear pure blue. *Geranium ibericum* also changes colour when the light fades. It often looks quite steely blue, like the night sky, writes Hill: "The loss of red improves some of the geraniums, changing the rather tawdry violet of *Geranium ibericum*, sometimes to a steely blue that matches the night sky."

Geranium 'Ivan'

(*G. psilostemon* × *G.* ×*oxonianum*?)

Height:	60 cm
Position:	Sun, partial shade
Flower:	Warm magenta-red with black eye and black veins. 4.5 cm
Season:	Midsummer
Propagation:	Division, basal cuttings

Geranium 'Ivan' is a hybrid similar to *G. psilostemon* in a lower-growing version and with larger flowers. (See plate of *G. psilostemon* and hybrids on page 107.) The hybrid comes from the Belgian Ivan Louette, who has also given us *G.* 'Philippe Vapelle' and *G.* 'Terre Franche.'

Other

In the catalogue for 1999 from the De Bloemenhoek nursery (now closed), they stated regarding *G.* 'Ivan': "When we were in the process of naming *Geranium* 'Philippe Vapelle', many years ago now, we got a plant from a *G. psilostemon*, which did not sow itself. Naturally we planted it, and because it reached 70 cm, unusually for such a plant, it was given the name of its breeder. He was also the breeder of 'Terre Franche' and 'Philippe Vapelle'." In Coen Jansen's catalogue, it states that *G.* 'Ivan' is a "medium-high selection from the Belgian

'*kluizenaar*' Ivan Louette." As I am an extremely curious person, I naturally wanted to know what a "*kluizenaar*" is. Coen Jansen explained that Ivan Louette is a hermit, an eccentric who is completely absorbed in plants—a somewhat unlucky turn of phrase, I think. Fortunately, you can be mad about plants without being a hermit and an eccentric.

Geranium 'Johnson's Blue'

(*G. himalayense* × *G.* ×*pratense*)

Height:	40 cm
Position:	Sun, partial shade
Flower:	Blue-violet. 4–5 cm.
Season:	Early summer
Propagation:	Division, rhizomes (no seed, the plant is sterile)

Geranium 'Johnson's Blue' is a hybrid that originated in Wales in the garden of A. T. Johnson (see "Other", below). The plant dates from 1950. It is often incorrectly sold as *G. himalayense*; however, you can easily see the difference between this species and 'Johnson's Blue'. One of the main differences is that the latter has yellowish stamens, while the stamens of *G. himalayense* are very dark (see plate on page 63).

When 'Johnson's Blue' is in full flower with its large, blue-violet flowers, you can look at it and think that as soon as it has finished flowering you ought to divide it up and plant it in lots of other places in your garden. Then in August when you see the plant after it has finished flowering, you just can't understand why you gave it such a prominent place in the garden, because it falls to the side and is so boring to look at.

That's what it's like with *G.* 'Johnson's Blue'; its weak point is that it just cannot remain upright. Don't hesitate, therefore, to cut this geranium down before it reaches this stage. The plant will soon respond with a new mound of green leaves and flowers often follow.

Other

A. T. Johnson lived in the Conway valley of north Wales. He had a large group of light blue *G. pratense* in his garden, and they fascinated Dutchman Bonne Ruys. He asked if he could have seeds from the plants, and when they germinated at home in Holland, among the seedlings was one that was clearly not a pure pratense geranium. It had a completely different stature from its siblings, and its flowers were also different; they were large and lavender-blue.

As *G. pratense* very seldom crosses with

Above: *Geranium* 'Jolly Bee' is an incredible plant. Here in October, as I write this caption, it is still in full bloom. I have planted *G.* 'Jolly Bee' in partial shade with *Hosta* 'Golden Tiara'.

other species of geranium, this was like finding a needle in a haystack. And in this case, Bonne Ruys being an expert, you could say it was a "tailor" who found the "needle".

Bonne Ruys was, in fact, a nurseryman, so he put the seedling into production and started selling it in 1950 under the name *G. pratense* 'Johnson's Blue'. Later it was discovered that the "father" of the plant must have been *G. himalayense*.

How on earth did this Dutch nurseryman get to know the Welsh former schoolteacher Arthur Tysilio Johnson (1873–1956)? Probably because Johnson wrote books about his garden and thus attracted many visitors, who wanted both to see his garden and to learn about the labour-saving plants he wrote so much about. In his short book, *Labour Saving Plants*, A. T. Johnson shows how plants can be used not just to provide beauty, but also to prevent weeds. Johnson particularly valued geraniums for both purposes, so his garden contained many different types. Two of the species,

G. endressii and *G. versicolor*, crossed and formed hybrids. Johnson chose two of the most attractive, which were then sold by his good friend Walter Ingwersen (see page 73). Both plants are still available. They are called *G. ×oxonianum* 'Rose Clair' and *G. ×oxonianum* 'A. T. Johnson'.

In addition to the book mentioned above, Johnson also wrote *A Garden in Wales* (1927), *A Woodland Garden* (1937) and *The Mill Garden* (1949).

Geranium 'Jolly Bee'

(*G. wallichianum* 'Buxton's Variety' × *G.*?)

Height:	50 cm
Position:	Sun, partial shade
Flower:	Deep blue with just a hint of red, whitish centre, purple veins and black stamens. 5 cm
Season:	Entire summer
Propagation:	Very careful division? Stem cuttings?

Geranium 'Jolly Bee' was found by nurseryman Marco van Noort in Warmond, near Leiden in Holland, and has recently gone on sale. The plant, which is a seedling from *G. wallichianum* 'Buxton's Variety' ('Buxton's Blue'), is also similar to its parent in both its marbled leaves and in its pretty,

G. 'Jolly Bee'

almost pure blue flowers. But *G.* 'Jolly Bee' is much better than *G. wallichianum* 'Buxton's Variety', as it flowers for much longer and has much greater growing power. I got my 'Jolly Bee' at the beginning of May this year, and as it was just recovering from its journey from Holland, it started flowering around 1 June. Now, at the time of writing at the end of August 2003, there is still no sign it intends to stop. The small stem with leaves, which is all it was on arrival, has developed into a close, lush plant that often sends out a flowering stem into neighbouring plants.

In the middle of July, I cut some of the stems into sections and potted them to see if you could propagate *G.* 'Jolly Bee' using stem cuttings. But it's as if this "jolly bee" is

Here are two beauties with delicate pink flowers.
Left: *G.* 'Joy'
Below: *G.* 'Kahlua'

so happy, it can't stop flowering. The small stem sections produce new flowers as fast as I can cut them off, and I tell the plant that it should be using its power to form roots and not flowers. Now I have realized that I cannot cope with the cuttings, so it is unlikely any new *G.* 'Jolly Bee' will come out of this experiment.

Geranium 'Joy'

(*G. lambertii* × *G. traversii* var. *elegans*)
Height: 40 cm
Position: Sun
Flower: Delicate pink with dark veins. 3 cm
Season: Entire summer
Propagation: Careful division, stem cuttings

Geranium 'Joy' has got the wrong parents for my conditions, which is a pity, as this plant is exceptionally beautiful. The hybrid, which comes from Alan Bremner, is named after Joy Jones, co-author with Trevor Bath of *The Gardener's Guide to Growing Hardy Geraniums* (1994) and chairman of the

Hardy Geranium Group of the Hardy Plant Society, England (see Address List). The leaves are marbled, and the flowers are shell-shaped and a delicate pastel pink.

As neither of the parents is hardy here in Denmark, I cover them well for the winter and then hope for the best.

Geranium 'Kahlua'

(*G. sessiliflorum*? × *G. traversii*?)
Height: 25 cm (mine is approximately 10 cm)
Position: Sun, partial shade
Flower: Delicate pink. Sepals look like a brown star in the light-coloured centre. 1.5 cm
Season: Midsummer
Propagation: Basal cuttings

Geranium 'Kahlua' is, in all likelihood, a cross of *G. sessiliflorum* subsp. *novaezelandiae* and *G. traversii* var. *elegans*. I have not been able to find any information about the parents of this hybrid, but it looks very similar to *G.* 'Chocolate Candy' and

G. 'Pink Spice', and it is believed that those are the parents of these two hybrids.

Geranium 'Kahlua' is very attractive with its brown leaves with a silvery sheen due to the small hairs that make it soft and velvety. The small light pink flowers are single, just as with *G. sessiliflorum* and *G. traversii*. It was also decided in 2001 that crosses between these two species should be called *G. ×antipodeum*. This means that the correct name for *G.* 'Chocolate Candy' is *G. ×antipodeum* 'Chocolate Candy' (and the same for *G.* 'Pink Spice'). Unfortunately, these hybrids are not hardy in my garden. I understand that in the south and the northwest of the United Kingdom they tend to come through the winter, but where winters are cold and wet it is best to treat them as annuals.

Geranium 'Kashmir Blue'

(*G. pratense albiflorum* × *G. clarkei* 'Kashmir White')
See page 55.

G. 'Khan'

Geranium 'Khan'

(*G. sanguineum* × *G. wlassovianum?*)

Height:	50 cm
Position:	Sun
Flower:	Dark magenta with dark veins. 4.5 cm
Season:	Midsummer
Propagation:	Division, stem cuttings

Geranium 'Khan' appeared as a seedling in the late 1980s in the garden of Allan Robinson, in England. The plant was right next to a colony of *G. wlassovianum*, but it was clear to Robinson that it was not a pure *G. wlassovianum* as the young plant began to show characteristics of *G. sanguineum*, of which there was one growing in the vicinity. The next year the plant had flowers that were very similar to those of *G. sanguineum* but with bold dark veins, resembling those in *G. wlassovianum* flowers. However, many people doubt that this is actually a hybrid between *G. sanguineum* and *G. wlassovianum*, as both species are very unwilling to cross with other species of geranium.

Geranium kishtvariense

Height:	50 cm
Position:	Shade or partial shade
Flower:	Shiny magenta with veins, white star-shaped centre and black stamens. 4 cm
Season:	Midsummer
Propagation:	Division, seed

Geranium kishtvariense forms low-growing, loose clumps. It spreads by means of thin rhizomes. The point where the leaf stalk, or petiole, joins the stem swells up, and this is a characteristic of the species. Unfortunately, this species, with its attractive large flowers, is very difficult to cultivate. It cannot cope with drought and must be covered during the winter.

Geranium kishtvariense was collected in Kashmir. The name refers to the valley where the species was found in 1978. The person who discovered it was the plant hunter Roy Lancaster.

A geranium which is very similar to *G. kishtvariense*, and which is also from Kashmir, is *G. rubifolium*. It is slightly taller and similarly not winter hardy. The species name *rubifolium* means "blackberry leaf".

Geranium koraiense

Height:	50–60 cm
Position:	Sun, shade
Flower:	Mauve with a dense network of purple veins, white centre. 3 cm
Season:	Midsummer
Propagation:	Difficult to propagate. That is all I can find out about it.

Geranium koraiense comes from Asia, and the species has only just been introduced for

G. kishtvariense

garden use. Bleddyn and Sue Wynn-Jones from the Welsh nursery Crûg Farm Plants brought it home with them from a plant expedition to South Korea. The plant is supposed to grow like *G. psilostemon*. The indented leaves are marbled green and light green. The flower stems are up to 1 metre long. Plants require well-drained ground. I do not know whether or not *G. koraiense* is hardy, although a Dutch catalogue describes the species as a large, winter-hardy plant.

Geranium koreanum

Height:	40 cm
Position:	Partial shade
Flower:	Magenta with purple veins, white centre. 4 cm
Season:	Midsummer
Propagation:	Seed

Geranium koreanum is a relatively new species from Korea. Mark Fillan, an employee at the Spinners Nursery, found the plant in South Korea around 1990. Bleddyn and Sue Wynn-Jones from Crûg Farm Plants subsequently also collected seeds from the plant on a trip to South Korea.

The leaves, which are indented and marbled, sit on long stems and turn attractive colours in the autumn. In full sun the plant become pale, writes Peter Yeo.

Reading the report from Bleddyn and Sue Wynn-Jones in the magazine for members of The Hardy Plant Society (Spring, 1998), I can see that the plant grows together with, among others, *Actaea simplex*, which is fully hardy in the garden. This might suggest that *G. koreanum* would also come through the winter. I know that the species has survived the winter in the garden of one of my friends in southern Jutland, in Denmark.

Above: *Geranium ×lindavicum* 'Apple Blossom' (synonym 'Jenny Bloom') is from Alan Bloom of Bressingham.

Geranium lambertii

Height: 30–45 cm
Position: Partial shade
Flower: Delicate pink with purplish
                red veins, purplish red centre,
                and black stamens. 3–4 cm
Season: Midsummer
Propagation: Seed; 'Swansdown' comes true
                from seed

Geranium lambertii (synonym *G. grevilleanum*) is a plant from the Himalayas with creeping growth and long stems, which often reach out into other plants. The flowers are unusually pretty, but unfortunately the plant is not hardy here in Denmark. I have been informed, however, that it survives the winter in Britain.

Alan Bremner has crossed the species with *G. swatense* and *G. procurrens*. A cross between the latter and *G. lambertii* originated around 1981 in the garden of Elizabeth Strangman, a well-known gardening writer and nursery owner. The hybrid, which is called *G.* 'Salome', has pale violet petals with dark violet veins, a dark violet centre and very dark stamens. *Geranium* 'Salome' can be propagated by means of stem cuttings.

Another known hybrid of *G. lambertii* is *G.* 'Joy'. *Geranium lambertii* takes its name from A. B. Lambert, a British botanist.

Varieties

Geranium lambertii 'Swansdown'
White-flowering form of the species, named by R. Clifton in 1979. There are pink veins on the white petals. The flower has a magenta centre and black stamens. The variety comes true from seed.

Geranium libani

Height: 40 cm
Position: Sun, partial shade
Flower: Pale violet with darker veins.
                4 cm
Season: Early summer
Propagation: Rhizomes, seed

Geranium libani takes its name from Lebanon, where it grows wild. The species, which is supposed to be hardy, is also found in Syria and in central Turkey. In the autumn, once the summer drought is over, *G. libani* "wakes up" and its shiny, indented leaves appear. In the spring, the plant has pale violet flowers, but once flowering is over it goes quiet and leaves a gap in the bed until its internal alarm clock rings in the autumn and new leaves appear. You therefore need to find something that can cover that space in the bed for the whole summer. You must also remember where the plant is and not accidentally dig it up. Underground, *Geranium libani* has a rhizomatous rootstock, but it does not spread so rapidly that the plant cannot be used in rock gardens.

Geranium ×lindavicum

(*G. argentum* × *G. cinereum*)
See page 52.

Geranium 'Little Gem'

(*G. ×oxonianum* × *G. traversii*)
Height: 15–20 cm
Position: Sun
Flower: Very bright magenta
Season: Midsummer
Propagation: Division

Geranium 'Little Gem' was created by Alan Bremner and introduced by Axletree Nursery. The hybrid is very similar to *G. ×riversleaianum* 'Russell Prichard', but is more compact, and the flowers are more intense in colour. Unfortunately, 'Little Gem' is not especially hardy. It needs excellent drainage and is therefore ideal for rock gardens.

Above: *G. macrorrhizum* is here being used as ground cover under trees in a large country garden.

Geranium macrorrhizum

Height:	30–45 cm
Position:	Sun or shade
Flower:	White, pink, magenta, purplish red. 2.5 cm
Season:	Early summer
Propagation:	Division, rhizomes, seed (but the varieties are not true to seed)

Geranium macrorrhizum grows wild in southern Europe in the Alps and Balkans, but can also occur in other locations in Europe. The sticky hairy leaves measure 10–20 cm and are more or less round and lightly indented. The plant smells distinctive (or stinks, according to your taste), and was formerly used for a number of different purposes. It has been used as a medicinal plant—the oil derived from it has been used for perfume, and in tanning processes.

Right: 1 *G. macrorrhizum* 'Album'
2 *G. macrorrhizum* 'Czakor' from 1975 (Hans Simon) and the pink *G. macrorrhizum* 'Ingwersen's Variety'.
3 *G. macrorrhizum* 'White-Ness' looks white in contrast to 'Album'.

Geranium macrorrhizum

G. macrorrhizum 'Album'

G. macrorrhizum 'Album'

G. macrorrhizum 'Bevan's Variety'

G. macrorrhizum 'Czakor'

G. macrorrhizum 'Ingwersen's Variety'

G. macrorrhizum 'Pindus'

G. macrorrhizum 'Snow Sprite'

G. macrorrhizum 'Spessart'

G. macrorrhizum 'White-Ness'

Geranium macrorrhizum is an incredibly hardy species, which makes good ground cover for difficult areas in the garden as it tolerates both shade and dryness. It can also be used in beds and borders in full sunlight. A variegated leaf variety is now available, *G. macrorrhizum* 'Variegatum'. It is pretty, in my opinion, but unfortunately it is slightly more fussy and demanding than the other varieties on the market.

Many macrorrhizum geraniums hold their leaves well over winter. Varieties that originate from plants in the northern part of their range lose their leaves before those from the southern part. Fortunately, the best varieties originate from the latter.

Macrorrhizum means "large root" and refers to the many stems that can sprout roots. Both the underground stems (rhizomes) and the plant's thick trailing stems can do this. Take a section of the stem and pot it, and you will soon have a new plant. It is as easy as that and it's another reason why *G. macrorrhizum* is a good for ground cover; because you can get a lot of plants quickly.

Varieties

Where the variety is low-growing, this is stated.

G. macrorrhizum 'Album'
White. The calyx is pink, as are the stamens, and at a distance it looks as if the flowers are pale pink. Collected by Walter Ingwersen in Bulgaria (see "Other", below).

G. macrorrhizum 'Bevan's Variety'
Magenta-red. Deep red calyx, which some people think clashes with the magenta-red colour of the petals.

G. macrorrhizum 'Czakor'
As for 'Bevan's Variety', but no visible veins on the petals. The plant is also supposed to be more compact than the species.

G. macrorrhizum 'Ingwersen's Variety'
Light pink. Pale green, slightly shiny leaves. Found in 1929 in Montenegro by Ingwersen (see "Other", below).

G. macrorrhizum 'Pindus'
30 cm. Magenta-red. The sepals are bright red so while the flowers are in bud it looks as if the plant has red fruits. Very low-growing variety, similar to G. ×cantabrigiense, partly because the plant is hairless. Collected in Greece by Bill Baker (see page 94).

G. macrorrhizum 'Snow Sprite'
White with green sepals. Resembles 'White-Ness'.

G. macrorrhizum 'Spessart'
White and very similar to 'Album'. From Dr. Hans Simon, who selected a macrorrhizum 'Album' with petals that overlap each other.

G. macrorrhizum 'Variegatum'
Magenta. Variegated leaves in yellow and green. Unfortunately, as with many other variegated perennials, it is not easy to grow.

G. macrorrhizum 'Velebit'
Difficult to tell apart from 'Pindus'.

G. macrorrhizum 'White-Ness'
White. This variety looks completely white, in contrast to 'Album'. The plant is actually an albino. Found in Greece in 1990 by Paul Matthews of Ness Botanic Garden, England, which belongs to the University of Liverpool.

Other

Geranium macrorrhizum is often used in large quantities for ground cover. 'Ingwersen's Variety' is very widely grown and performs well. It was also the first *G. macrorrhizum* I noticed—perhaps because as a Dane myself, I thought the name had a nice Danish ring to it. Over the years since, I have often come across the name Ingwersen in connection with geraniums, and eventually I became so curious to know something about this Ingwersen that I contacted Birch Farm Nursery, Ingwersen's nursery.

I talked to Ingwersen's son, Paul. He explained that his father, Walter Ingwersen, was born in Hamburg in June 1882, adding that he was the result of his father's third marriage—presumably so I wouldn't think he was very old! The famous gardening

Above left: The foliage of *G. macrorrhizum* displays its rich autumn colour.
Above: *G. macrorrhizum* 'Pindus' looks like it bears small fruits. However, they are only the plant's red sepals closed in a bud.

author Will Ingwersen was his older brother from Walter Ingwersen's first marriage.

Walter's father was a wine trader, and the family had roots in the Danish area of northern Germany, so the name probably does come from Denmark. However, the young Walter's mind turned to plants, not wine, to his father's great disappointment—a disappointment that made him practically throw Walter out of the house. He was given a small amount of money to set himself up in England, where he arrived in May 1902. In 1925, he moved into a house near where Birch Farm still stands today.

This place, Gravetye Manor, also has a history behind it, as it was here that the legendary William Robinson lived (see page 63 for details of Robinson and *G. himalayense* 'Gravetye'). Like many people with German-sounding names, Walter Ingwersen was interned as an alien during the First World War, but he was released in 1917 into the custody of the Royal Horticultural Society so he could work in its garden at Wisley. Walter Ingwersen died in 1960.

Right: *G. maculatum* 'Espresso'
Below right: The very white *G. maculatum* 'Album'.

Geranium macrostylum

Height:	35 cm
Position:	Sun, partial shade
Flower:	Pale pink with dark reddish centre or lavender-blue with dark veins. 2.5 cm
Season:	Early summer
Propagation:	Tubers

Geranium macrostylum is a pretty little geranium from Greece, Albania, southern Yugoslavia and Turkey. The flower is found in two versions, one pale pink, and the other lavender-blue. *Geranium macrostylum* spreads rapidly with small, oblong tubers to such an extent that it can be considered a nuisance, particularly in rock gardens. You can solve this problem by keeping it restrained in a pot.

After flowering, *Geranium macrostylum* goes underground and this is how it survives the dry summers common in the regions from where the species originates. By storing nutrients in its tubers, the plant is able to "switch itself off" until autumn, when new leaves appear, and grow rapidly when the spring rain brings excellent growing conditions. The species is hardy in Denmark, as I know from one of my plant friends.

Geranium maculatum

Height:	35–60 cm
Position:	Partial shade, tolerates sun if the soil is damp
Flower:	White, pink, pale mauve, purplish red, white centre. 3 cm
Season:	Early summer and often again later
Propagation:	Division, seed (the varieties are probably not true to seed)

Geranium maculatum comes from the eastern part of North America, where it grows in woodland, and arrived in Europe in 1732. It is generally known in the U.S.A. as the wild geranium. The species name means spotted. There is no evidence of this on the leaves of plants grown in gardens, although in the wild the leaves are said to be lightly spotted.

The leaves look like hands with seven fingers. I have also described *G. sylvaticum* leaves in the same way, but with *G. maculatum*, the cuts between the "fingers" look like they have been made with a craft knife. They are very clean and V-shaped, and the greater part of the margin is without any small notches.

The forests where *G. maculatum* grows have good nutrient-rich soil. The species, therefore, cannot tolerate a dry location in the garden. Plant it in the lightest part of a

woodland bed and give it plenty of compost.

Lately, a number of beautiful varieties have appeared in which the leaves are the most interesting feature. Some have brown or yellow leaves, and a new variety from Switzerland has foliage that turns orange in the autumn.

Varieties

Where I am unsure of the height, I have put a question mark (?).

G. maculatum 'Album'
50 cm. White. This plant has no anthocyanin pigment, so it is an albino. Its leaves are therefore very pale.

G. maculatum 'Beth Chatto'
60 cm. Light pink. Large, shiny flowers. This variety comes from well-known gardening author and nursery owner Beth Chatto.

G. maculatum 'Elizabeth Ann'
(?) Magenta. Very dark, chocolate brown leaves.

G. maculatum 'Espresso'
40 cm. Pale mauve. The leaves are chocolate

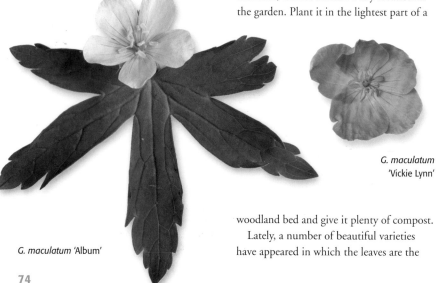

G. maculatum 'Album'

G. maculatum 'Vickie Lynn'

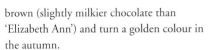

brown (slightly milkier chocolate than 'Elizabeth Ann') and turn a golden colour in the autumn.

G. maculatum 'Heronswood Gold'
(?) The leaves are yellowish. I do not know the flower colour.

G. maculatum 'Shameface'
(?)Reddish violet.

G. maculatum 'Spring Purple'
35 cm. Magenta. Compact plant, with deep red leaves during the spring. This variety is from the well-known Dutch garden designer Piet Oudolf.

G. maculatum 'Vickie Lynn'
40 cm. Mauve. The leaves, which are shiny green, turn completely orange in the autumn. This variety comes from Switzerland.

Other

Geranium maculatum is one of the cranesbills that are unable to survive if the garden is dry. In an article I read once about impulse purchases of perennials, the author explained that he was often tempted by lush plants with exotic flowers at nurseries—"and dear me, all it needed was a moist, well-drained spot in full sun", he jokingly wrote. He then went on to explain that, of course, he was unable to find such a spot when he got home with the beauty. Well, who does have such a spot? That was just what I thought when I read that *G. maculatum* can stand in the sun if the soil is moist.

The first *G. maculatum* I ever had I lost after a very wet winter. The plant, which was in a part of the garden that had been under water for a few days, must have rotted away. Therefore I don't dare put my *G. maculatum* in my marsh bed in the sun.

Geranium 'Madelon'

(*G. psilostemon* × *G.* ×*oxonianum*?)

Height:	80 cm
Position:	Sun, partial shade
Flower:	Dark mauve with burgundy eye and veins. 2 cm
Season:	Midsummer
Propagation:	Division, basal cuttings

Geranium 'Madelon' is a hybrid found in Holland and introduced by nurseryman Coen Jansen. He got the plant from one of his customers, who had found it in the garden. 'Madelon' is an old Dutch girl's name. *Geranium* 'Madelon' looks like a miniature *G. psilostemon*. It is a delightful and very long-flowering plant, livening up beds with its brilliant colours, which are not quite as "barbarically splendid" as *G. psilostemon*, to quote Ingwersen's description of this species ("…its fine big, cupped flowers of barbaric splendour").

Geranium maderense

Height:	100 cm
Position:	Frost-free greenhouse; a protected spot outside in the summer
Flower:	Deep pink, dark magenta centre and red stamens. 4 cm
Season:	Entire summer
Propagation:	Seed, which must be stored for a month or two

Geranium maderense comes from Madeira, hence its species name. It is the largest of the cultivated geraniums. The leaves are enormous, as much as 60 cm across. The stem, which has to bear the leaves, is like a small tree trunk. The aromatic leaves are highly indented, and their stems are brownish. The flower stems are closely covered with red glandular hairs, so the flowers seem extra red. The plant dies after flowering, though it may sometimes continue with side shoots.

Geranium maderense is the second largest geranium in the world. The largest is called appropriately enough *G. arboreum*, which means "tree-like"; it is 1.5 metres tall and grows in Hawaii.

Below: *Geranium ×magnificum* 'Blue Blood' has light green leaves, which make the flowers appear extra dark.

G. × magnificum
'Blue Blood'

G. × magnificum
'Rosemoor'

Geranium ×magnificum

(*G. ibericum* × *G. platypetalum*)

Height:	40–70 cm
Position:	Sun or partial shade
Flower:	Dark bluish purple with veins. 4–5 cm
Season:	Early summer
Propagation:	Division; as the plant is sterile, no seeds are produced

Geranium ×magnificum is a cross between *G. ibericum* and *G. platypetalum*. This plant, which has been known for over a hundred years, is sterile and has overtaken both its parents, under whose names it is often mistakenly sold. The round, indented and hairy leaves colour well in autumn. The plant tolerates dryness incredibly well and can grow virtually anywhere, although perhaps not in the deepest shade. It is

Below: *Geranium ×magnificum* 'Rosemoor' is one of the compact varieties which do not flop over.

occasionally seen alongside roads in residential areas or planted on traffic islands because of its ability to look after itself for years.

Geranium ×magnificum is one of the best known and most widely used cranesbills. It is a shame that it does not display its attractive, very dark bluish purple flowers throughout the summer. The type that is generally planted has, in addition to its relatively brief flowering season, the shortcoming that it flops over easily. However, you can now get much better varieties, which are lower growing and also in flower for longer.

Varieties

G. ×magnificum
70 cm. Bluish purple. Tall plant that easily topple.

G. ×magnificum '**Blue Blood**'
50 cm. Very dark bluish purple. The leaves are light green, which probably also makes the flowers seem very dark.

G. ×magnificum '**Peter Yeo**'
(Also known as *G. ×magnificum* Clone "C")

45 cm. Differs from the other varieties in having flowers that are bluer. The petals are also broader, and overlap. The large flowers appear in very great abundance.

G. ×magnificum '**Rosemoor**'
50 cm. Dark bluish purple. Flowers for a long period. One of the compact varieties which do not fall over.

G. ×magnificum '**Turco**'
40 cm. Very dark bluish purple. Smaller and fewer flowers than other varieties. The leaves look like those of *G. renardii*. Grows slowly. The plant is officially registered as a *G. platypetalum*, but according to Coen Jansen the plant is neither a G. *platypetalum* nor a *G. ibericum*, which is why he sells it as a *G. ×magnificum*.

Other

The name *Geranium ×magnificum* was given to the plant in 1961 by the Swede Dr. Nils Hylander, from Uppsala Botanical Garden. He wanted to build up a collection of geraniums and repeatedly received this geranium as a *G. platypetalum*. However, he

acquired the genuine *G. platypetalum* from different botanical gardens under various names. When he discovered that the plant was sterile, he compared it with *G. ibericum* and *G. platypetalum* and concluded that it had to be a hybrid of the two species. He could not discover when the hybrids had originated, but in a herbarium in the Botanical Museum in Uppsala he found one example from 1871, which had been collected in the botanical garden of Geneva.

Geranium makmelicum

See the Cinereum Group on pages 52–53.

Geranium malviflorum

Height:	30 cm
Position:	Sun
Flower:	Violet-blue with dark veins. 4 cm
Season:	Spring
Propagation:	Tubers

Geranium malviflorum originates from southern Spain and Morocco where it copes with the summer heat and drought there by withering away after flowering. The leaves, which are 10–15 cm wide and deeply indented, generally appear again in the autumn. The tubers of this species, with their reserves of food, make it able to grow rapidly and flower in the spring.

Of the geraniums that have tubers, *G. malviflorum* is the one with the largest leaves. The species is ideal for rock gardens, but can also be put in a sunny bed in well-drained soil. *Geranium malviflorum* has survived the winter for me, but I do not know if it is fully hardy.

Geranium 'Mary Mottram'

(*G. endressii* × *G. sylvaticum* 'Album') Low-growing and abundant in flowers. See page 125.

Right: A close look into *G.* 'Maxwelton'.
Far right: A leaf of *G. psilostemon*.
Below: *G.* 'Natalie', one of Alan Bremner's hybrids, dates from 1997.

Geranium 'Maxwelton'

(*G. psilostemon* × *G.* ×*oxonianum* 'Wargrave Pink')

Height: 50 cm
Position: Sun, partial shade
Flower: Warm magenta with small black eye
Season: Midsummer
Propagation: Division, basal cuttings

Geranium 'Maxwelton' resembles its "sister" *G.* 'Patricia', as both have flowers like

G. ×*monacense* 'Muldoon'

G. psilostemon, but in subdued colours. *Geranium* 'Maxwelton' grows very slowly. The plant was found by John Ross, a nurseryman in Scotland.

Geranium ×monacense

(*G. phaeum* × *G. reflexum*)

Height: 60–80 cm
Position: Shade, partial shade
Flower: Burgundy, pinkish violet. 2.5 cm
Season: Early summer and again after cutting back
Propagation: Division, rhizomes, seed

Geranium ×*monacense* is a hybrid that has arisen spontaneously in gardens. Its parents are the species *G. phaeum* and *G. reflexum*, which are very similar to one another, and *G.* ×*monacense* does look exactly like *G. phaeum*. *Geranium* ×*monacense* got its name from Dr. K. Hartz in 1921, when he found the hybrid in his garden in Munich. This city was called Monachium in Latin, and "monacense" means "resident of Munich".

It seems that the hybrid also arose at other times and places, as it is found in various versions. E. A. Bowles was writing about plants that were a mix of *G. phaeum* and *G. reflexum* as early as 1914.

One of the versions or varieties of *G.* ×*monacense* has very bold, dark patches at the base of the leaf indents. It often appears in catalogues as *G. punctatum*, or *G. phaeum* 'Punctatum'. Both names are wrong; the plant is correctly called *G.* ×*monacense* 'Muldoon'.

As with *G. phaeum*, *G. reflexum* originates from southern Europe. The latter has flowers in clear pinky red or dark violet colours.

Varieties

Where I am not sure of the height, I have put a question mark (?).

G. ×*monacense* '**Breckland Fever**'
(?)Mauve. Flowers from early spring to July.
G. ×*monacense* '**Claudine Dupont**'
(?)Dark pink with grey-blue zone. The leaves have reddish brown patches.
G. ×*monacense* '**Muldoon**'
70 cm. Burgundy. Bold dark patches at the base of the leaf indentations.

Geranium 'Natalie'

(*G. clarkei* 'Kashmir White' × *G. saxatile*)

Height:	45 cm
Position:	Sun
Flower:	Blue-violet with reddish tinge, whitish centre and black stamens. 3 cm
Season:	Early summer
Propagation:	Division, basal cuttings

Geranium 'Natalie' is a hybrid created by Alan Bremner. It was introduced in 1997 by Judith Bradshaw of Catforth Gardens. The hybrid is named after her granddaughter.

Geranium 'Natalie', which is very abundant in flower, begins to bloom early in the season at the same time as *G. macrorrhizum*. The leaves are very indented, and their lobes are pointed (see photograph on the page opposite).

Geranium nepalense

See under *G. thunbergii*, page 127.

Geranium nervosum

Height:	30–45 cm
Position:	Sun, partial shade
Flower:	Pink or magenta with purple veins and small white eye. 2–4 cm
Season:	Entire summer
Propagation:	Careful division, seed

Geranium nervosum (synonym *G. strigosum*) is North American and very variable in appearance. The shape of the highly indented leaves may vary, as may the colour and size of the flowers. The plant is aromatic and has sticky hairs. Generally, it sends out a single flower stem, which branches at the top.

For a long time American gardening writers mistakenly called this species *G. incisum*, under which name it was therefore sometimes listed in catalogues. *Geranium incisum* is a name that is more

correctly a synonym for another North American cranesbill, namely *G. oreganum*. Many of the more unfamiliar geraniums are best suited to wild gardens, as their flower stems are quite floppy. This is not the case with *G. nervosum*. This species has a nice, upright growth habit and holds its flat flowers prettily over its leaves. It thus earns a place in any bed; moreover it can also cope with rather dry spots in the shade under trees and shrubs.

G. 'Nicola'

Geranium 'Nicola'

(*G.* ×*oxonianum* × *G. psilostemon*)
See under *G.* 'Patricia', page 95.

G. 'Nimbus'

Geranium 'Nimbus'

(*G. clarkei* 'Kashmir Purple' × *G. collinum*)

Height:	60 cm
Position:	Sun
Flower:	Blue-violet with dark veins and light centre. 2.5 cm
Season:	Midsummer
Propagation:	Division

Geranium 'Nimbus' was found in 1978 as a seedling in the University Botanic Garden, Cambridge, in England, and the plant was introduced in 1990 by David Hibberd's nursery, Axletree Nursery.

The leaves are an attractive yellowish green when they appear in the early spring. Later, the filigree-like leaves turn a lusher green. The star-shaped flowers and the fine-cut foliage give the plant a light, delicate appearance. The plant produces seeds, and its progeny resemble *G.* 'Nimbus' but do not inherit the same genes, so the seedlings cannot be called *G.* 'Nimbus'.

Geranium nodosum

G. nodosum

G. nodosum 'Simon'

G. nodosum 'Svelte Lilac'

G. nodosum 'Whiteleaf'

G. nodosum 'Svelte Lilac'

G. nodosum 'Whiteleaf'

Dark magenta with white edge. I assumed that the leaves had a white edge when I saw the name, but this is not the case. The name refers to the property where the plant originated. Lionel Bacon, who wrote a number of articles about geraniums, lived at "Whiteleaf".

Geranium oreganum

Height:	60 cm
Position:	Sun
Flower:	Deep pink, very reddish, light centre. 5 cm
Season:	Midsummer
Propagation:	Division, seed, rhizomes

Geranium oreganum comes from North America. The highly indented leaves are similar to those of *G. pratense*. The large flowers are slightly transparent and quite red. A lovely geranium that deserves to be far more widely used.

Geranium nodosum

Height:	30 cm
Position:	Shade or partial shade
Flower:	Light pink, pink, dark magenta with white edge. 2.5–3 cm
Season:	Entire summer
Propagation:	Division, rhizomes, seed (the varieties are not true to seed)

Geranium nodosum grows wild in mountain areas in France, Italy and the former Yugoslavia. The leaves, which are divided into three or five lobes, are particularly pretty. They are very smooth and shiny.

Geranium nodosum is an especially useful plant for shady areas, as it is a woodland plant that flowers all summer long. It can therefore take over from most other shade-bed plants, which flower in the spring. As the plants are low growing, they can be placed at the front of a bed or border.

Varieties

G. nodosum 'Simon'
Pink.

G. nodosum 'Svelte Lilac'
Light pink, with a metallic sheen and purple veins. The edge of the flower is slightly wavy, as there is a little notch in each petal. My absolute favourite.

G. nodosum 'Swish Purple'
Deep magenta colour, velvety. Grows slowly.

G. oreganum

Geranium orientali-tibeticum

Height:	20 cm
Position:	Sun
Flower:	Dark pink with large white centre. 2.5 cm
Season:	Midsummer
Propagation:	Tubers

Geranium orientali-tibeticum originates from southwestern China. Its main attraction is its leaves, which are marbled yellow and green. The species is closely related to *G. pylzowianum*, which also has rhizomes with tubers. This is actually the main failing of the species, as the rhizomes with their tubers run all over the place, so the plant shoots up everywhere.

Geranium orientali-tibeticum is a rock garden plant, but don't plant it in the middle of your rock garden, as that is a place where it is fairly difficult to dig out unwanted growth without destroying something else. It is better to plant it at the edge or at the front of the bed in well-drained soil. You could also grow it in a pot.

Other

Geranium orientali-tibeticum was introduced around 1914 by the Veitch nursery, in England, which was famous for employing its own plant hunters to find novelties for the market. In total twenty-two plant hunters were employed over a period of sixty-five years. The penultimate was the most famous: E. H. Wilson (1876–1930), who in 1903 discovered *G. orientali-tibeticum*. Of the thousand or so species Wilson found, he is most famous for introducing *Davidia involucrata* (the dove, or handkerchief, tree) and *Lilium regale* (the regal lily).

Geranium 'Orion'

(Seedling from *G.* 'Brookside')

Height:	70 cm
Position:	Sun, partial shade
Flower:	Deep blue, quite pure in colour, purple veins and white eye. Up to 6.5 cm
Season:	Midsummer
Propagation:	Division

Above: On this early morning in the middle of June, *G.* 'Orion' resembled large, blue poppies.

Geranium 'Orion', which is a seedling from *G.* 'Brookside', was found by a Dutch nurseryman, Brian Kabbes, late in the 1990s. *Geranium* 'Orion' has very large flowers that are darker than those of *G.* 'Brookside'. Otherwise, the plant resembles its parent.

As the flower stems are rather long, it is best to plant this geranium next to sturdy perennials, such as asters, which can give the stems a little support.

G. 'Orion'

Below: Summer is here! This picture was taken on 17 June, and the cranesbills are now filling the garden with their flowers. In the foreground is *G. ×oxonianum* 'Julie Brennan', which can also be seen in close-up, to the right.

G. ×oxonianum 'Julie Brennan'

Geranium ×oxonianum

(*G. versicolor* × *G. endressii*)

Height:	30–80 cm
Position:	Sun or partial shade
Flower:	White, all shades of pink and burgundy, with and without a network of veins on the petals. 3–4 cm
Season:	All summer
Propagation:	Division, basal cuttings and some varieties have rhizomes, seed (but the varieties do not come true)

All the many varieties of *Geranium ×oxonianum* can be enjoyed in the garden from early in the year, when the plants form dense green mounds, until late in the autumn, when the final bloom bids us farewell. Apart from summer-flowering annuals, I cannot think of a plant that can compete in terms of abundance of blossom.

The varieties of *G. ×oxonianum* have many uses. As they tolerate some shade, grow quickly and are easy to propagate, they can be used for ground cover. If the geraniums are to cover the ground beneath trees and shrubs, they must be planted at the side that faces the light to ensure flowering.

If you are looking for a good neighbour for one or more perennials, then choose *G. ×oxonianum*, as you can always find a variety to suit. The number of shades these geraniums are available in is huge. The flowers of *G. ×oxonianum* may be small and almost double, or like large, flat cups, or the petals may be so far apart that they look like stars.

The leaves also show variation. One of the parents, *G. versicolor*, has a maroon patch at the base of each indentation on its leaves, and this has been inherited by *G. ×oxonianum*. Some varieties have the inherited patch extended to cover almost the whole leaf, while in others the patch can hardly be seen, so the leaf can appear entirely green.

After the main flowering in June, some varieties may need cutting back but they will soon be back on track again, with fresh leaves and new flowers. When and whether it is necessary to cut back will depend on the year. If the plants have been "on the go" early, most varieties benefit from cutting back in July. On the other hand, if there has been a very late spring, it is not certain that cutting back will be necessary. The plants themselves will make it clear (see photograph 1).

Some *G. ×oxonianum* have inherited the characteristic from *G. endressii* of the flowers becoming darker as they get older—they fade in reverse. This gives an excellent effect.

Unfortunately, *G. ×oxonianum* has also inherited the enormous fertility of its parents and thus produces many seeds. The varieties cross with each other, with the parent species and occasionally with *G. psilostemon*, among others. Take a walk with a pair of scissors and cut off the seed heads once in a while. However, the double forms 'Southcombe Star' and 'Southcombe Double' are sterile.

Above: 1 If you fail to cut *G. ×oxonianum* down at the right time, the plant solves the problem itself. It lays its stems out to the side and pushes up fresh green topgrowth in the middle. You can then cut off all the abandoned stems for there is already a new, flowering plant in the making.
2 *G. ×oxonianum* 'Hollywood' has large, attractive, delicately coloured flowers.
3 Both stamens and petals have developed from leaves. However, the tissue in the stamens can suddenly "forget" its job, so instead of stamens forming, petal-like growths are produced and this is how semi-double flowers develop. This example is *G. ×oxonianum* 'Southcombe Star'.

Geranium ×oxonianum

G. ×oxonianum 'A.T. Johnson'

G. ×oxonianum 'Ankum's White'

G. ×oxonianum 'Armitageae'

G. ×oxonianum 'Breckland Sunset'

G. ×oxonianum 'Bregover Pearl'

G. ×oxonianum 'Claridge Druce'

G. ×oxonianum 'Coronet'

G. ×oxonianum 'David McClintock'

G. ×oxonianum 'Dawn Time'

G. ×oxonianum 'Frank Lawley'

G. ×oxonianum 'Hexham Pink'

G. ×oxonianum 'Hollywood'

G. ×oxonianum 'Julie Brennan'

G. ×oxonianum 'Kate Moss'

G. ×oxonianum 'Katherine Adele'

G. ×oxonianum 'Kingston'

G. ×oxonianum 'Königshof'

G. ×oxonianum 'Lace Time'

G. ×oxonianum 'Lambrook Gillian'

G. ×oxonianum 'Miriam Rundle'

Geranium ×oxonianum

G. ×oxonianum 'Old Rose' 1

G. ×oxonianum 'Old Rose' 2

G. ×oxonianum 'Pearl Boland'

G. ×oxonianum 'Phoebe Noble'

G. ×oxonianum 'Phoebe's Blush'

G. ×oxonianum 'Rebecca Moss'

G. ×oxonianum 'Rosemary'

G. ×oxonianum 'Rødbylund'

G. ×oxonianum 'Sherwood'

G. ×oxonianum 'Southcombe Double'

G. ×oxonianum 'Southcombe Star'

G. ×oxonianum 'Stillingfleet Keira'

G. ×oxonianum 'Sue Cox'

G. ×oxonianum 'Summer Surprise'

G. ×oxonianum 'Susie White'

G. ×oxonianum 'Thurstonianum'

G. ×oxonianum 'Trevor's White'

G. ×oxonianum 'Wageningen'

G. ×oxonianum 'Walter's Gift'

G. ×oxonianum 'Wargrave Pink'

G. ×oxonianum 'Waystrode'

G. ×oxonianum 'Winston Churchill'

Above: Geraniums are so robust that children and dogs can roam freely in the garden. If stems break, the plant soon shoots up again. Here Freja takes a nap next to *G. ×oxonianum* 'Bregover Pearl'.

Varieties

Unless otherwise stated, the height is 40–50 cm; where I am not sure of an individual plant's height when fully grown, this is indicated by a question mark (?).

G. ×oxonianum 'A. T. Johnson'
Low-growing, around 30 cm. Light pink, silvery. The flowers become a little darker with age. Light green leaves. From A. T. Johnson (see page 66), gardener and schoolteacher who lived in Wales. See also 'Rose Clair'.

G. ×oxonianum 'Ankum's White'
White. The first white *G. ×oxonianum* to retain its whiteness in the heat. Earlier attempts to create a white 'Rose Clair' have resulted in plants whose flowers were only white in temperatures below 20ºC. In warmer temperatures, the flowers were pink. From Coen Jansen, Holland.

G. ×oxonianum 'Armitageae'
Magenta with veins. Narrow petals.

G. ×oxonianum 'Breckland Sunset'
Deep pink with dark purple veins. From The Plantsman's Preference nursery, 1998.

G. ×oxonianum 'Bregover Pearl'
Delicate pastel pink, pink veins and blue stamens. The flower is slightly transparent. If I was forced to choose just one *G. ×oxonianum*, it would be this one.

G. ×oxonianum 'Claridge Druce'
70 cm. Dark pink with network of dark veins. Extremely robust plant that is said to be best for ground cover where it can have plenty of space, as it can easily overrun other plants. For more about this variety see "Other", page 93.

G. ×oxonianum 'Coronet'
Deep pink with white centre. The petals are narrow, and it looks as if the flower has a few extra ones. However, these are actually petaloid stamens (converted stamens).

G. ×oxonianum 'David McClintock'
60 cm. Mauve with purple veins. Very narrow petals spaced far apart, so the flower looks like a star. Occasionally forms double flowers.

G. ×oxonianum 'Dawn Time'
35 cm. White-pink with network of veins. Large part of the leaf is red-brown.

G. ×oxonianum 'Frank Lawley'
35 cm. Pale pink in a mellow colour.

G. ×oxonianum 'Hexham Pink'
60 cm. Pink with a lot of violet. Large-flowered. Powerful, vigorous plant.

G. ×oxonianum 'Hollywood'
70–80 cm high, but dense. Pale pink with magenta veins, very large flowers. A splendid plant, which looks fabulous—hence its name.

G. ×oxonianum 'Armitageae'
& Tradescantia ×andersoniana 'Concord Grape'

G. ×oxonianum 'A.T. Johnson'

G. ×oxonianum 'Ankum's White'

G. ×oxonianum 'Frank Lawley'

*G. ×oxonianum 'Susie White'

1 Sometimes *G. ×oxonianum* 'Southcombe Star' forms almost double flowers.
2 Some varieties of *G. ×oxonianum* seem to reverse the usual fading, as the flowers become darker with age. The contrast in 'Old Rose' is particularly noticeable.
3 *G. ×oxonianum* 'Wageningen' and 'Walter's Gift'.
4 *G. ×oxonianum* 'Phoebe Noble', which is a very dark magenta in colour, comes from Vancouver Island, where Phoebe Noble has her garden.

Many varieties of *G. ×oxonianum* form both plain leaves and those that are mottled at the base of indentations. **Left and centre** are from *G. ×oxonianum* 'Bregover Pearl', while on the **right** is a leaf from *G. ×oxonianum* 'Katherine Adele'.

G. ×oxonianum 'Julie Brennan'
60 cm. Deep pink with burgundy veins. Very large flowers. Good robust plant.

G. ×oxonianum 'Kate Moss'
Pale pink with magenta veins.

G. ×oxonianum 'Katherine Adele'
(?) Pale pink with purple veins. A large part of the leaf is maroon. Seedling from 'Walter's Gift'. From America, Daniel Hinkley, Heronswood Nursery (see page 106).

G. ×oxonianum 'Kingston'
White with magenta veins.

G. ×oxonianum 'Königshof'
Dark mauve, heavily veined. Very large flower. From the Sarastro Nursery in Austria.

G. ×oxonianum 'Lace Time'
White, heavily veined, very similar to *G. versicolor*. Its leaves are tinged with yellow.

G. ×oxonianum 'Lambrook Gillian'
Pale pink with purple veins.

G. ×oxonianum 'Miriam Rundle'
35 cm. Dark magenta. In the spring, the plant forms a yellowish green mound.

G. ×oxonianum 'Old Rose'
Pale pink, pink, with dark pink veins. The flowers "fade in reverse", getting darker with age.

G. ×oxonianum 'Pearl Boland'
Similar to 'Old Rose' but the flowers have a pearly sheen.

G. ×oxonianum 'Phoebe Noble'
Very dark magenta. The darkest of all the varieties listed.

G. ×oxonianum 'Phoebe's Blush'
Pale pink flowers "fade" to dark pink. No veins.

G. ×oxonianum 'Rebecca Moss'
Large, shiny, pale pink flowers. No veins. Vigorous plant.

G. ×oxonianum 'Rose Clair'
Warm pink flowers that change colour only slightly with age. An extremely common plant in Danish gardens and until I saw the English perennial catalogues I thought that "she" was an only child, but there are actually a large number of sister plants as you can see from this list. In actual fact, the original 'Rose Clair' and 'A. T. Johnson' are very rare, as it has been a number of years since they were sold at Ingwersen's nursery (see page 73). Walter Ingwersen described 'Rose Clair' as: "A clear rose-salmon with just a trace of veining and similar habit to *G. A. T. Johnson*".

The National Collection at Cherry Hinton Hall in Cambridge, England, has the two plants reckoned to be 'Rose Clair' and 'A. T. Johnson'. My 'A. T. Johnson' originates from the latter, but not my 'Rose Clair', so I have decided not to include an image of it. Innumerable oxonianum geraniums have been sold as 'Rose Clair', and many Danish gardens contain a variety with very dark cyclamen red flowers. It is this plant that a large nursery (Bakkely, now closed) chose and distributed as 'Rose Clair'.

A group of foreign nurserymen found one of these 'Rose Clair' at Rødbylund Nursery and in recognition of the fact that it was not the real 'Rose Clair', promptly rechristened the plant *G. ×oxonianum* 'Rødbylund'. As the owner of Rødbylund Nursery, Denmark, said, it would have been more appropriate to christen it "Bakkely".

G. ×oxonianum 'Rosemary'
(?) Shiny pastel pink, blue stamens and greenish centres. No veins.

G. ×oxonianum 'Rosenlicht'
Very deep pink. From Heinz Klose in Germany. The flowers are often mistaken for those of 'Phoebe Noble'.

G. ×oxonianum 'Rødbylund'
See 'Rose Clair', above.

G. ×oxonianum 'Sherwood'
(?) Pale pink with narrow widely-spread petals. Star-shaped flowers. Occasionally forms double flowers.

G. ×oxonianum 'Southcombe Double'
Brilliant pink flowers. Sometimes the plant forms double flowers (petaloid stamens, see 'Coronet'). Small star-shaped flowers, sometimes resembling a pompon. Unfortunately, this variety is very slow-growing. Sterile.

G. ×oxonianum 'Southcombe Star'
Bluish pink with veins. Sometimes forms double flowers (petaloid stamens, see 'Coronet'). Small star-shaped flowers. More vigorous and robust than the previous variety. Sterile.

G. ×oxonianum 'Spring Fling'
35 cm. Pink. Small flowers. The interesting thing about this variety, although I've never seen it myself, is that it is the first oxonianum with variegated leaves. The leaves are cream-coloured with shades of yellow and pink. The centre of the leaf is green, with dark spots between the leaf sections. Unfortunately, the leaves grow greener during the summer. It dates from 2000.

G. ×oxonianum 'Stillingfleet Keira'
60 cm. Deep pink with veins. Small flowers. Sometimes forms double flowers.

G. ×oxonianum 'Summer Surprise'.

G. ×oxonianum 'Trevor's White'

G. *×oxonianum* 'Sue Cox'
(?) Deep pink with small veins. Small, double flowers of the same type as 'Coronet' and 'Southcombe Double'. Very pretty dark-patterned leaves similar to those of 'Walter's Gift'. Slightly creeping.

G. *×oxonianum* 'Summer Surprise'
60 cm. Dark mauve, a few dark veins with a cream-coloured centre. A vigorous plant with large flowers.

G. *×oxonianum* 'Susie White'
Pale pink with purple veins.

G. *×oxonianum* 'Thurstonianum'
60 cm. Magenta with veins of a darker mauve. Narrow, often twisted and widely-spread petals. Fairly large, star-shaped flowers, approx. 3 cm. Petaloid stamens (see 'Coronet'). Sometimes forms double flowers.

G. *×oxonianum* 'Trevor's White'
White with blue stamens. Undergoes colour changes. The flowers turn pale pink in warmer weather and with age. Also sold as *G. endressii* 'Album'. A plant I bought called *G. ×oxonianum* 'White Form' is exactly like 'Trevor's White'.

G. *×oxonianum* 'Wageningen'
Vibrant dark pink with orange undertones. It's difficult to describe this colour, but I can well understand how this plant caught the eye of Dr. Hans Simon, a German plant hunter and nurseryman, who spotted it in 1987 as a wild seedling outside the botanical garden in the Dutch town of Wageningen.

When I exhibited my geraniums at a large flower show at Clausholm in 2001, an enormous number of people pointed to the 'Wageningen', wanting to know its name.

G. *×oxonianum* 'Walter's Gift'
Pale pink with veins. A large part of the leaf is a beautiful maroon.

G. *×oxonianum* 'Wargrave Pink'
60 cm. Pink, not true pink but with a blue tinge. A particularly robust, vigorous plant.

G. *×oxonianum* 'Waystrode'
White with purple veins. A very vigorous plant. Vibrant but not too intense.

G. *×oxonianum* 'Winscombe'
Pale pink fading to dark pink.

G. *×oxonianum* 'Winston Churchill'
A reddish dark pink. Very vibrant. Slow growing.

Other

The hybrid of *G. versicolor* and *G. endressii* which was chosen to be the prototype, or typical example of a hybrid between these two species, was named in Oxford in 1960. It was called 'Claridge Druce' after the botanist who discovered it in 1900. The name was chosen by Graham Stuart Thomas and the Director of the Oxford Botanic Garden, which Thomas was visiting at the time. In light of the fact that the prototype was named in Oxford, Peter Yeo chose the name "oxonianum" as the generic term for all hybrids of *G. versicolor* and *G. endressii*. The name was first published in Yeo's book *Hardy Geraniums* in 1985.

Earlier in this entry I wrote that the *G. ×oxonianum* varieties can be used as ground cover—a term I actually have some difficulty with. I see before me expanses of absolutely identical plants—a type of "green asphalt" often used in public places as a labour-saving device. Where large areas need to be covered, these always look better with a green carpet rather than paving or gravel to reduce the need for weeding.

Gardens rarely have enormous areas that simply need to be covered, and it is possible to use ground cover plants in a different way to create a great deal more variation. Use varieties of *G. ×oxonianum* alongside other herbaceous perennials that give good ground coverage. The many colours of the different varieties mean we can create miniature living pictures using only ground cover plants.

Those of you who are not gardening fanatics perhaps think that one pink *G. ×oxonianum* is enough, but we need lots of different shades and textures in order to be able to "paint" with plants. An added bonus of a large number of varieties is that it satisfies a primitive urge to collect and compare—we are, after all, descended from hunters and gatherers.

What I like best about the oxonianum type of geranium is that they grow in a beautifully relaxed manner. They unfold as clouds of flowers, often gently stretching their "arms" out round their neighbours. They add a romantic aspect to the garden, and with their inclusion the perennial border will form a harmonious whole, rather than military-style rows of flowers.

Geranium palmatum

Height:	Up to 120 cm
Position:	Greenhouse or a sunny spot outside in the summer
Flower:	Bright mauve, darker in the centre. 3–4 cm
Season:	Midsummer
Propagation:	Seed

Geranium palmatum (synonym *G. anemonifolium*) must be cultivated as a pot plant here, as it is not hardy. It is like *G. maderense* from Madeira, and may survive outside in gardens that experience mild winters as long as it is planted in a sheltered spot.

The heavily indented leaves can reach up to 35 cm in width, and the plant produces a lot of flowers. The flower stems, like those of *G. maderense*, have magenta hairs. The seeds germinate easily.

This species has been grown in Europe since the 1700s and has generally been known as *G. anemonifolium*. However, this name was first published two years after *G. palmatum*, which is why the latter name takes precedence.

Geranium palustre

Height:	40 cm
Position:	Sun
Flower:	Warm deep pink with purple veins and small white eyes. 3 cm
Season:	Midsummer
Propagation:	Division, seed

Geranium palustre grows wild in eastern and central Europe. The species name means "growing in marshy areas", so you might think this plant is difficult to grow. This is by no means the case. It can cope with full sun and fairly dry soil in gardens.

The plant grows in a sprawling manner and forms long runners, which do not take root. The strongly indented leaves are quite small (5–10 cm), smooth on top and shiny underneath. The flowers are a brilliant pink, but not as harsh a colour as the flowers of *G. psilostemon* and its hybrids. Probably one of the best uses for these cranesbills is if you can find a place in the bed between plants that finish flowering early and around which *G. palustre* can weave its long runners, giving these herbaceous perennials "new flowers". It is also the natural choice for wild gardens, where the plants can have their fling.

Other

In plant hunter Bill Baker's garden, which was cold and damp, *G. palustre* thrived and the species produced a seedling that was much better than its parent. The seedling produced flowers just above its foliage, unlike *G. palustre* with its long wobbly stems.

In the first instance, Bill Baker called the seedling 'Palustre Plus' and thought that *G. gracile*, which grew alongside, was part of it. However, Peter Yeo has decided that the plant is a hybrid of *G. sylvaticum* and *G. palustre*. The hybrid has bright magenta flowers with strong purple veins. Bill Baker

christened it *G.* 'Tidmarsh' after the village where he lived.

Bill Baker became interested in alpine plants when he spent his summer holidays in Austria shortly after the Second World War, and this prompted him to join the Alpine Garden Society. He travelled to the Dolomites, northern Italy and Switzerland with the Society. These trips taught Bill Baker a lot about plants and stimulated his interest in geraniums. On one of these early expeditions, he found a *G. phaeum* var. *lividum* that had large flowers. The plant later produced a very beautiful seedling, which David Hibberd's Axletree Nursery began selling under the name *G. phaeum* var. *lividum* 'Joan Baker'; the plant was named after Baker's wife.

Near Wengen in Switzerland, Bill Baker discovered an attractive, delicate pink form

of *G. sylvaticum*. Baker intended to christen it "Wengen", but others had a better name—*G. sylvaticum* 'Baker's Pink'. (The plant may, however, be sold under the unofficial name *G. sylvaticum* 'Wengen'.) Bill Baker also collected plants in Greece. In the Pindus mountain range, he found a very low-growing, compact *G. macrorrhizum*, which grew by a bright *G. subcaulescens*. This geranium was given the name *G. macrorrhizum* 'Pindus'.

Bill Baker explains that he found a *G. nodosum* with a dark centre part and white edges to its dark pink petals, in a forest in the Alps. Peter Yeo writes in his work on hardy geraniums that Bill Baker always chose seedlings from the plant with the darkest flowers and this was how he created *G. nodosum* 'Whiteleaf'.

However, in June 1993 Dr. Lionel Bacon

that are frequently called "eye-catching". Plants with delicate pastel pink flowers look good next to those with silver or grey leaves; no one is afraid of using this particular colour combination. Sometimes, however, I feel a little more "devil-may-care", and *G.* 'Patricia' is just right for more unusual compositions. Situated next to plants with deep orange flowers or leaves containing a hint of burgundy, *G.* 'Patricia' can give a bed a truly exotic appearance. A hybrid that is very similar to *G.* 'Patricia' is *G.* 'Nicola', which differs by having narrower well-spaced petals that form a star shape.

Geranium peloponnesiacum

Height:	60 cm
Position:	Sun, partial shade
Flower:	Pale violet with dark veins. 4 cm
Season:	Early summer
Propagation:	Division, seed

Geranium peloponnesiacum originates in Greece. It was introduced to gardens in 1972 by Richard Gorer, who collected seeds from this species in the Pindus mountain range. The leaves, which have deep indentations and are wrinkled, disappear once flowering has finished, only to reappear in the autumn. This species "sleeps" during the summer in the same way as *G. macrostylum* and *G. tuberosum*, which are also from the Mediterranean region. This is how they survive the dry conditions and the heat. *Geranium peloponnesiacum* has a thick rhizome containing nutrients, which allows rapid growth during the short spring when there are optimum growing conditions. The best time to divide the plant is during its rest period.

  Geranium peloponnesiacum is one parent of the hybrid *G.* 'Stephanie', and as this appears to be fully hardy in my own garden, my theory is that *G. peloponnesiacum* is hardy in most regions.

wrote in the Alpine Garden Society's Bulletin (the members' newsletter) that he had been removing all paler forms of *G. nodosum* from his garden for the past twenty-five years. He likes to call the now predominant colourful dark forms "Whiteleaf", after his house. Perhaps we can divide the honours for *G. nodosum* 'Whiteleaf' between the two men. It seems natural to believe that at some point Bill Baker gave Lionel Bacon a piece of his *G. nodosum*, and that the dark forms in Lionel Bacon's garden descended from this.

  Bill Baker died on 16 March 2001.

Geranium papuanum

See *G.* 'Bertie Crûg' on page 48.

Geranium 'Patricia'

(*G. endressii* × *G. psilostemon*)

Height:	75 cm
Position:	Sun, partial shade
Flower:	Light magenta with a lot of pink; dark burgundy eye. 4 cm
Season:	Entire summer
Propagation:	Division, basal cuttings

Geranium 'Patricia' is a hybrid created by Alan Bremner. The plant combines the best characteristics of both parents. It flowers for considerably longer than *G. psilostemon* and is also much smaller. *Geranium endressii* is "responsible" for this, while the warm magenta-red flowers with a dark eye are clearly derived from *G. psilostemon*. *Geranium* 'Patricia' is one of those plants

Geranium phaeum

G. phaeum 'Album'

G. phaeum 'Calligrapher'

G. phaeum 'Chocolate Chip'

G. phaeum 'David Bromley'

G. phaeum 'Joan Baker'

G. phaeum 'Lily Lovell'

G. phaeum 'Margaret Wilson'

G. phaeum 'Samobor'

G. phaeum 'Variegatum'

Above: *G. phaeum* 'Album' in the morning sun.

Above: *G. phaeum* 'Variegatum' with *Hosta* 'Patriot.'
Below: *G. phaeum* 'Chocolate Chip'

Geranium phaeum

Height: 40–110 cm. Unless otherwise stated varieties are around 80 cm

Position: Sun or shade

Flower: Dark red, burgundy, maroon, mauve, white. 2.5–3 cm

Season: Early summer and again after cutting back

Propagation: Division, rhizome, seed (varieties are not true to seed)

Geranium phaeum grows wild in southern and central Europe. Further north, it has strayed into the wild from gardens. Its common name is dusky cranesbill. The species name means "brownish" and probably refers to the maroon flowers. The very large leaves, up to 20 cm across, are indented and at the base of each indentation is often a dark stain or large spot. The leaves and stems are covered in hairs.

Geranium phaeum is extremely hardy, can withstand dry conditions and is almost evergreen. The mass of leaves form dense, vigorous mounds, making it excellent as a ground-cover plant. You can transform a boring, shady and dry corner into something exciting simply by using different varieties of *G. phaeum*.

There are varieties with variegated leaves

96

in yellow, white and burgundy, and some with a particularly eye-catching dark border. *Geranium phaeum* is best known for being able to tolerate deep shade, but it can also cope with some sun.

The petals are slightly reflexed, which gives the flower its characteristic appearance. The varieties with light-coloured flowers will brighten up shady borders alongside ferns and hostas.

Geranium phaeum can be cut back once it has finished flowering. This prevents your garden being overrun by seedlings the following year, and the plant soon forms a new dense mound. *Geranium phaeum* is particularly well suited to wild gardens or informal gardens. The offspring can easily colonize a large area, and these vigorous plants will not be overrun by weeds.

Above: *Geranium phaeum* 'Joan Baker' with a hairy Braun's holly fern, *Polystichum braunii*.

Varieties

G. phaeum 'Album'
As the name suggests, this variety is white. Found in Switzerland and first sold in 1946.

G. phaeum 'Calligrapher'
Pale violet. The base and edges of its ruffled petals are dark violet in colour. The centre has a clear violet ring. Very similar to 'David Bromley'. The leaves have maroon stains or patches.

G. phaeum 'Chocolate Chip'
110 cm. The darkest variety. The plant, which forms a pretty, round column, is extremely sculptural. From California.

collector Bill Baker, who died in 2001, found a pretty *G. phaeum* var. *lividum* on one of his many collecting trips. An attractive seedling from this trip was named after his wife, Joan.

G. phaeum 'Lily Lovell'
1 m. Very dark violet. Created and introduced by Trevor Bath (co-author of *The Gardener's Guide to Growing Hardy Geraniums*), who named it after his mother.

G. phaeum 'Lisa'
Dark red flowers. The pale green leaves have a pretty yellow section in the centre. From Coen Jansen in Holland.

G. phaeum 'Little Boy'
40 cm. Burgundy, leaves of one colour. From Coen Jansen in Holland.

G. phaeum 'Margaret Wilson'
60 cm. Bluish purple. Very pretty leaves with yellow veins look as though they have been spray-painted yellow.

G. phaeum 'Raven'
60 cm. Dark chocolate brown flowers.

G. phaeum 'Rose Madder'
60 cm. Brownish red flowers, which in my opinion is a strange colour, so I do not grow this plant any more. Others think that it is quite unique.

G. phaeum 'Samobor'
Burgundy. The leaves are fantastic. They have a broad black-red band. The plant was found in 1990 near Samobor in Croatia by Elizabeth Strangman (known primarily for her hellebores). 'Saturn' is supposed to be an enhanced version, but it is impossible to tell the difference.

G. phaeum 'Stillingfleet Ghost'
Pale grey. This variety comes from the Stillingfleet nursery. The ghostlike colour of the flowers is probably what inspired David Hibberd when he named this variety, which he actually tested. The leaves are plain green.

G. phaeum 'Taff's Jester'
Burgundy. The leaves are marbled with yellow either over their entire surface or on one half only. Mine only produce yellow-variegated leaves occasionally.

G. phaeum 'Conny Broe'
Burgundy. Shortly after it starts to appear like any ordinary green plant in the early spring, the leaves change colour, to become almost chequered with green and yellow. Towards the end of the summer, the leaves start to turn green again. See "Other", on page 99, and "A Visit to Coen Jansen", page 40.

G. phaeum 'David Bromley'
Pale violet with violet edges. Enhanced form of 'Calligrapher'.

G. phaeum 'Golden Samobor'
Maroon. Particularly interesting foliage, like 'Samobor' but the leaves also have a bright yellow marking. From Coen Jansen.

G. phaeum 'Golden Spring'
50 cm. Pale burgundy with a magenta ring and white centre. In spring the plant has yellow leaves; these later turn green.

G. phaeum var. lividum 'Joan Baker'
Pale mauve with small purple streaks around the centre of the flower. The plant

Left and far left: This marble-leaved *G. phaeum* has been given the name 'Conny Broe'.

Below left: *G. phaeum* 'Samobor' with *Hosta* 'Frances Williams'.
Below right: *G. phaeum* 'Lily Lovell'

G. phaeum 'Variegatum'

Burgundy. Variegated leaves. The leaves have splashes of cream, yellow, white and some red. The plant tends to be most variegated when new growth appears in the spring and after cutting back.

Other

An unbelievable number of new geranium hybrids have appeared on the market over the past few years. Someone jokingly compared the purchase of new geraniums with buying a new computer—even before you have got it home, there is a new, improved version being launched. It's not quite as bad as that, but if you want plants you can be sure are hardy and will always be among the classics, *G. phaeum* is the obvious choice.

G. 'Philippe Vapelle'

Go into the garden on a spring morning after a hard ground frost, which damages plants and worries gardeners, and you may encounter a chirpy-looking *G. phaeum* standing green and erect, as though nothing had happened.

Geranium phaeum and *G. reflexum*, which are closely related, can be crossed. The hybrids have been given the name *G. ×monacense*. You may also encounter the name *G. ×monacense anglicum*, where *G. phaeum* var. *lividum* has been crossed with *G. reflexum*.

A few years ago a couple visited one of our Open Garden events with a *G. phaeum* that they had brought to show me because they didn't think I had it in the garden. My eyes certainly widened, because I had never before seen this particular *G. phaeum*, with almost chequered leaves. The first thing I did was send pictures of it to Coen Jansen in Holland, who was also very enthusiastic about it. He subsequently received a plant for testing, and I wrote about the new *G. phaeum* in the Danish gardening publication *Haven* (March 2002). The plant has now been given the name *G. phaeum* 'Conny Broe', which was chosen by the couple who produced the original plant. Nobody knows where this plant originated, but it definitely deserves a name.

Geranium 'Philippe Vapelle'

(*G. platypetalum* × *G. renardii*)
Height: 35 cm
Position: Sun
Flower: Dark bluish purple. 3.5 cm
Season: Early summer
Propagation: Division

Geranium 'Philippe Vapelle' is a pretty plant with soft grey-green leaves. The bluish purple petals are slightly separated from one another, giving the flower a star-like appearance. Tolerates dry conditions. (See *G. renardii*, under "Other" on page 111.)

Geranium platyanthum

Height: 50 cm
Position: Partial shade, sun
Flower: White, pale violet. 3 cm
Season: Early summer and again later on
Propagation: Division, seed

Geranium platyanthum (synonym *G. eriostemon*) is native to northeast Asia and a belt stretching from eastern Siberia to Tibet, China, Korea and Japan.

It is an extremely hairy plant with large pale green leaves, which are divided into between five and seven lobes. The flowers are often described as being a rather boring violet colour. *Geranium platyanthum* is therefore probably most suitable as a foliage plant in a sunny position or in partial shade beneath trees and in wild gardens. The leaves take on further attractive hues in the autumn.

There is a white-flowered version, which is lower growing. This is called *G. platyanthum* f. *albiflorum*.

Other

There will soon be a variety of *G. platyanthum* available from garden centres. The plant originated in the garden of one of Coen Jansen's customers. On my visit to him, he talked enthusiastically about the plant, which has splendid pure blue flowers. The variety has not yet been given a name.

Geranium platypetalum

Height: 40 cm
Position: Sun
Flower: Dark bluish purple. 3–4.5 cm
Season: Early summer
Propagation: Division, seed

Geranium platypetalum originates in Turkey and the Caucasus. This is a hairy plant with somewhat rounded, patchy leaves. In spring 2003 I bought a *G. platypetalum*, which was

collected in Georgia, in the Caucasus, by the renowned plant hunter and plantsman Roy Lancaster. 'Georgia Blue', which was the name eventually given to this *G. platypetalum*, is characterized by vigorous dark violet blooms.

G. platypetalum is rarely found in garden centres. Plants with this name usually turn out to be *G. ×magnificum*, a sterile hybrid. (*G. ×magnificum* = *G. platypetalum* × *G. ibericum*.)

Geranium pogonanthum

Height: 45–60 cm
Position: Sun, partial shade
Flower: Pale pink with white centre and magenta stamens. 3 cm
Season: Late summer
Propagation: Division, seed

Geranium pogonanthum is native to southwest China and north and western Burma. The flowers have reflexed petals and resemble small cyclamens. The leaves have deep indentations and are prettily marbled with yellowish green. The species is quite difficult to place in the garden, as the flowers are easily overrun by neighbouring plants. As it is sensitive to dry conditions, the best place to plant it is in a shady spot in the rock garden, but in an elevated position so its splendid flowers can clearly be seen.

Other

Geranium pogonanthum was introduced in 1956 by Frank Kingdon Ward (1885–1958), the "Blue Poppy Man", as he is sometimes referred to in the United Kingdom. It was Kingdon Ward who discovered the Himalayan blue poppy (*Meconopsis betonicifolia*) in 1925.

Geranium pogonanthum was one of the last plants Frank Kingdon Ward discovered, and for a long time it was assumed to be *G. yunnanense*. Peter Yeo discovered the error during the 1980s and corrected the plant's name to *G. pogonanthum*.

Geranium pratense

G. pratense 'Album'

G. pratense 'Bittersweet'

G. pratense 'Cluden Sapphire'

G. pratense 'Eben'

G. pratense var. stewartianum 'Elizabeth Yeo'

G. pratense 'Galactic'

G. pratense Midnight Reiter

G. pratense 'Mrs Kendall Clark'

G. pratense 'Plenum Album'

G. pratense 'Plenum Caeruleum'

G. pratense 'Plenum Violaceum'

G. pratense 'Silver Queen'

G. pratense 'Striatum'

G. pratense Victor Reiter

G. pratense 'Wisley Blue'

Right: *G. pratense* 'Plenum Album' was looking this good the first year I had it. In order to keep it that way, I have to give it water and compost, and propagate it carefully by division.
Below: *G. pratense* 'Striatum'

Geranium pratense

Height:	60–80 cm, but up to 125 cm if the plant has optimum conditions (sunny and moist)
Position:	Sun or slight shade
Flower:	Blue, white, pink, pale magenta; some have bold stripes. 3–4 cm
Season:	Early summer and again after cutting back
Propagation:	Division, basal cuttings, seed (not all varieties are true to seed)

Geranium pratense grows wild in the United Kingdom and much of Europe and Asia. The name of the species means "growing in meadows" and it is commonly known as the meadow cranesbill, but it does grow in other locations. It can survive by roadsides and in other dry areas. In parts of northern Europe it has become naturalized where it has escaped from gardens. The flowers are generally blue in colour, but wild varieties can also be white and pale blue. The large leaves have deep indentations and appear open, almost like filigree work.

The species adapts easily to ordinary garden soil, provided that the site is not bone dry. Compost can be added to retain soil moisture. If the plant is given enough water, it is also less inclined to be susceptible to mildew, which is one of the weaknesses of this particular species. The other is the copious amount of seeds, which can produce far too many plants if the withered flowers are not removed in time. If you choose to grow only varieties of this species that have double flowers, you can avoid the problem of self seeding, as double varieties of *G. pratense* are sterile.

Lately, some exciting varieties have been launched onto the market. Some have burgundy-coloured leaves, and there is one that is supposed to be almost mildew resistant.

As the varieties of *G. pratense* make vigorous plants, their neighbours should not be low, slow-growing perennials, but more like perennial phlox or astilbes, for example. These also prefer a sunny position and soil that is not too dry.

Below: *Geranium pratense* var. *stewartianum* 'Elizabeth Yeo' in the early morning. Peter Yeo, taxonomist and author of a major work, *Hardy Geraniums*, named this *G. pratense* after his wife.

Varieties

The height is given only for the lowest-growing plants.

G. pratense 'Album'
White.

G. pratense 'Bittersweet'
Pale pink with dark veins and black stamens.

G. pratense 'Cluden Sapphire'
Dark sapphire blue.

G. pratense 'De Bilt'
Creamy white flowers on upright stems. From Dutchman W. Ploeger.

G. pratense 'Eben'
Pale blue. This plant, which is supposed to be very nearly mildew resistant, has been found in the wild. It comes from the Sarastro nursery in Austria.

G. pratense 'Galactic'
Milky white. Large flowers, with petals overlapping slightly. This particular variety is albino, which means the plant does not contain any of the pigment anthocyanin.

G. pratense 'Mrs Kendall Clark'
Pale sky blue with white veins. Comes true from seed.

G. pratense 'Plenum Album'
70 cm. White double flowers. It seems as though the colours in the very thin veins of the petals are blurred towards the centre, with small reddish purple patches.

This variety is more demanding than the other doubles. It requires water and nutrients, and needs to be divided carefully now and again to keep it in good condition.

G. pratense 'Plenum Caeruleum'
60 cm. Lavender-blue with reddish centre. Its pretty double flowers are slightly looser compared with the pompon-like 'Plenum Violaceum'.

G. pratense 'Plenum Violaceum'
60 cm. Dark violet with a pink blush. The flowers are perfectly shaped pompons. Flowers later than previous varieties. A cheerful, old-fashioned variety that brings an air of romance to a garden.

G. pratense **Reiter cultivars**

60 cm. These cultivars, which have burgundy leaves, all come from a single seedling that Victor Reiter, an American plant collector who ran a nursery in California during the 1970s, found in a batch of sown seeds.

Reiter collected the seeds produced by this plant, sowed them and then selected the seedlings with red leaves, which he used for breeding. By selecting the best red-leaved plants generation after generation, he was able to create a seed strain. A seed strain refers to a variety that is propagated from seed, and only the best seedlings are chosen to bear the name of the variety. The name of the seed strain must not be used in single inverted commas. Others have since continued Victor Reiter's work with the result that today there are many red-leaved varieties available.

As these can be propagated from seeds as well as by micro-propagation or division, there may be a great, sometimes a very great, difference between two plants with the same name. It is therefore not surprising that there is great confusion regarding the naming of these varieties. Experts are currently trying to sort out the situation, but this will take some time, as the plants are now widespread.

At present, it might be best to regard the naming of varieties with red leaves as tentative, which is why the names below are written without single quotes. Unfortunately, the red-leaved varieties grow slowly, and towards the summer the leaves lose some of their burgundy colour and become greener.

Black Beauty is from Nori Pope, Hadspen Garden (2002) and is only 45 cm high. This plant is reckoned to retain the dark colour of its leaves better than other varieties. Plants are micro-propagated.

Midnight Reiter has beetroot-coloured leaves with a greyish underside and dark blue flowers.

Purple Haze is a seed strain from Plantworld Seeds (launched in 2000). The catalogue states that seedlings can vary in height and leaf colour, and flowers may be blue, violet or magenta. Finally, it recommends that you should destroy seedlings with green leaves.

Purple Heron, which has particularly dark leaves and dark violet flowers, is a low-growing variety.

Victor Reiter has burgundy leaves with deep indentations and dark violet-blue flowers.

G. pratense 'Rose Queen'

60 cm. Delicate pink with purple veins.

G. pratense 'Silver Queen'

Violet-blue or whitish. The colour depends on the weather. Warm and sunny: whitish. Wet weather results in bluish violet flowers. Its stamens are black.

G. pratense var. *stewartianum* 'Elizabeth Yeo'

Pale magenta-red. Translucent flowers that appear as early as May. The plant is a variety of the European *G. pratense* from Kashmir. Named by Peter Yeo (see page 33).

G. pratense 'Striatum'

(Also sold under the name 'Splish Splash') White with lavender-blue streaks, white, lavender-blue. A "three-in-one" variety, as some flowers are pure white, others are lavender-blue and some are white with lavender-blue streaks and patches. I don't think any two of the two-tone flowers are identical. There is now a version with pink rather than lavender-blue patches, which is called 'Janet's Special'.

G. 'Prelude'

Geranium 'Prelude'

(*G. albiflorum* × *G. sylvaticum*)

Height:	45 cm
Position:	Shade, partial shade
Flower:	Pale violet. 2 cm
Season:	Early summer
Propagation:	Division

Geranium 'Prelude' is, as the name suggests, an early bloomer—prelude means "introduction" in French. This hybrid covers itself in small pale violet flowers. Plant in a woodland bed.

Geranium procurrens

Height:	30 cm
Position:	Shade, sun
Flower:	Dark bluish purple with a black centre and black veins and stamens. 2.5 cm
Season:	Late summer
Propagation:	The stems put down roots wherever they touch the ground; seed

Geranium procurrens is native to the Himalayas but is not hardy in northern Europe. British gardeners write that the plant can easily prove too vigorous for smaller gardens, as it grows quickly and forms new plants wherever the stems touch the ground in a similar way to strawberries. Therefore, *G. procurrens* can cover a large area under trees and bushes with lightning speed.

Geranium procurrens is a parent plant to *G.* 'Ann Folkard', *G.* 'Anne Thomson' and *G.* 'Dilys'. The species name is well chosen, as *procurrens* means "moving forwards". The plant was given its name in 1973 by Peter Yeo.

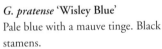

G. pratense 'Wisley Blue'
Pale blue with a mauve tinge. Black stamens.
G. pratense 'Yorkshire Queen'
White with magenta veins.

Other

In the garden I have a seedling from Midnight Reiter (to acquire seeds, see Address List). I selected the best plants from the seedlings produced, throwing away the plants with green leaves or leaves that were less red—there are always some that are only "eleven o'clock" (as opposed to as darkly red as Midnight).

In general, it is possible to say that varieties of *G. pratense* are surprisingly consistent when grown from seed, but *G. pratense* can be crossed with other varieties. The best-known hybrid is *G.* 'Johnson's Blue'.

Above: *Geranium pratense* 'Plenum Violaceum' is a charming variety. In this picture, it blends well with *G.* ×*oxonianum* 'Frank Lawley' to create a romantic atmosphere.

In his book *The Explorer's Garden* (1999), Daniel Hinkley, owner of the famous Heronswood Nursery in the U.S.A., writes of *G. pratense* 'Striatum', which does not come completely true from seed, that you can recognize the seedlings that are not true to variety by their reddish leaf stems. It is nice to know that you don't need to look after them until you see the flowers, but can discard them immediately.

It is strange that this type has produced many double varieties, when there are only very few double geraniums. There are, however, other single-flowered varieties that give the impression of being a double by having a few extra petals, and all of these are varieties of *G.* ×*oxonianum*.

Geranium psilostemon and hybrids

G. psilostemon

G. psilostemon 'Bressingham Flair'

G. 'Ann Folkard'

G. 'Anne Thomson'

G. 'Eva'

G. 'Ivan'

G. 'Madelon'

G. 'Maxwelton'

G. 'Nicola'

G. 'Patricia'

G. 'Red Admiral'

Geranium psilostemon

Height: Up to 120 cm
Position: Sun or slight shade
Flower: Increasingly warm magenta-
               red with black eye and veins.
               4 cm
Season: Midsummer
Propagation: Division, basal cuttings, seed

Geranium psilostemon is native to northeast Turkey and the southwest Caucasus. It is also called *G. armenum*. This makes a large vigorous plant with leaves up to 20 cm across. Once the plant starts growing in the early spring, the new shoots that appear are blood red in colour.

Geranium psilostemon is an eye-catching addition to flowerbeds, although it can be a challenge to find good neighbours; plants with flowers of pale citron yellow or delicate pink tones are possibilities. If your nerves are up to it, you could try using plants that produce orange or burgundy flowers.

Varieties

G. psilostemon 'Bressingham Flair'
A subtler colour than is usual for this species. A seedling originating from Alan Bloom of the Bressingham nursery and introduced in 1973.

G. 'Red Admiral'

are some terms that were used. Magenta is definitely not included in The Royal Horticultural Society's Colour Chart.

Personally, I quite like the colour magenta and *G. psilostemon*. Luckily I am not alone in this and there have been numerous attempts to cross *G. psilostemon* with other plants in the genus in order to transfer the colour or the black eye to new varieties.

The hybrids are sterile and the following have *G. psilostemon* as one parent:

'Ann Folkard' (spontaneous cross with *G. procurrens*), see page 47.

'Anne Thomson' (cross with *G. procurrens*), see page 47.

'Eva' (cross with *G. pratense*), see page 59.

'Ivan' (*G. psilostemon* × *G. ×oxonianum*), see page 66.

'Madelon' (cross with *G. ×oxonianum*), see page 75.

'Maxwelton' (*G. psilostemon* × *G. ×oxonianum* 'Wargrave Pink'), see page 78.

'Nicola' (cross with *G. ×oxonianum*), see page 79.

'Patricia' (cross with *G. endressii*), see page 95.

'Red Admiral' (cross with *G. sylvaticum* 'Baker's Pink'), see page 110.

Above: *Geranium psilostemon* with *Salvia ×superba* 'Rubin'.

A leaf of *G. psilostemon*.

Other

Much has been said about the fiery colours of *G. psilostemon*. E. A. Bowles (1865–1954), a well-known gardener with a sense of humour who loathed magenta-red, wrote of psilostemon: "The magnificent black eye saves it from being one of the worst astringents of the vision in the whole garden, but such a colour reacts on my retina much as alum does on my tongue." His comments on magenta were: "*G. sylvaticum* in some forms comes perilously near a similar shade."

Reginald Farrer (famed for *G. farreri* and a contemporary of Bowles) also despised the colour magenta. Because two such prominent gardeners could not abide the colour, the use of plants bearing magenta-red flowers was regarded as a sign of bad taste. English nurseries therefore set about coining other terms when describing plants with magenta-red flowers: crimson, carmine, purple-red, cerise, rosy red, fuchsia purple and cyclamen

Below: *Geranium pylzowianum*, which has tuberous roots, spreads quickly underground, so it must be planted somewhere where you can control it and remove unwanted growth.

Above: Here *G. pylzowianum* has "invaded" a small blue speedwell.

Geranium pylzowianum

Height:	25 cm
Position:	Sun
Flower:	Pink with slightly darker veins, small green eye and cream-coloured stamens. 2.5 cm
Season:	Early summer
Propagation:	Tubers, seed

Geranium pylzowianum, which comes from China, must be kept on a short rein in the garden. This pretty geranium with elegant, small and deeply indented leaves spreads rapidly through a flower bed. You can easily see why when you dig the plant up. The species has long thin threads with beads (nodules) every 2–3 cm. These are rhizomes with tubers that can each produce a new plant. Even though the natural position for *G. pylzowianum* is the rock garden, planting it right in the centre of your bed is a mistake, as you will be unable to remove unwanted plants without destroying something else. Plant it below your rock garden or at the edge of the bed in well-drained soil. Alternatively, this species can also be grown in pots.

Geranium pylzowianum was discovered in 1910 by William Purdom (see page 60) and introduced by the Veitch nursery (see page 82).

Geranium pyrenaicum

Height:	30 cm
Position:	Sun, shade
Flower:	White, mauve, bluish purple, violet. 1.5 cm
Season:	All summer
Propagation:	Seed

Geranium pyrenaicum has "very sharp elbows" and also small round jagged leaves. It is a weed-like plant that scatters enormous amounts of seeds, which germinate and grow quickly, steamrollering other plants in the garden. You should therefore be extremely careful if you allow this species into your garden. It is indigenous to the Mediterranean countries, but it has now spread throughout most of Europe, including Scandinavia. The plant is also called the Pyrenean cranesbill. It has mauve flowers and is found here and there on grass verges and other uncultivated areas. It has spread to the wild from gardens and is often imported in grass seed mixtures.

Varieties

G. pyrenaicum f. *albiflorum*
White. Large star-shaped flowers. Just as productive as the species where seeds are concerned.

G. pyrenaicum 'Bill Wallis'
Dark bluish purple. Very pretty, but is capable of spreading like a weed. The name is often misspelled 'Bill Wallace'.

Left: *G.* 'Red Admiral' is the only "pure red" psilostemon hybrid.
Below: 'Red Admiral' interacts wonderfully with *Anthemis tinctoria* 'Sauce Hollandaise'.

G. pyrenaicum 'Isparta'

Violet with white centre. Large plant (60 cm) producing large flowers. This variety was discovered in Turkey by Peter Yeo in 1989.

Geranium 'Red Admiral'

(*G. psilostemon* × *G. sylvaticum* 'Baker's Pink')

Height:	60 cm
Position:	Sun
Flower:	Deep pink with black veins and a black eye. 4.5 cm
Season:	Midsummer
Propagation:	Division, basal cuttings

Geranium 'Red Admiral' is pure red in colour, unlike other hybrids of *G. psilostemon*, which are more often magenta-red with a bluish tinge. The flowers are red and black; it is probably for this reason it was called 'Red Admiral', after the butterfly of the same name, whose wings are also marked with red and black.

Unfortunately, I have been unable to trace the creator of this exquisite hybrid. Luckily, *G.* 'Red Admiral' is a dynamic, strong-growing plant.

Other

Often when I get new geraniums, I don't know what they will look like. Normally, the plants have been bought from catalogues with a description but no pictures of the plant. This was the case with my *G.* 'Red Admiral'. I can remember wondering "how much redder is it than psilostemon? Is it pinker or is it almost magenta in colour?" I created pictures of it in my mind in order to imagine what I could plant around it to make an attractive display. Soon I was moving this and that around to produce the optimum effect. Creating a bed with plants whose colours and shapes you have yet to see is mental exercise, and one of the things I like best about gardening.

Other people, long before me, have obviously also felt the same, as I found a quote from *Pot Pourri From A Surrey Garden* (1897) by Mrs. C. W. Earle: "Half the interest of a garden is the constant exercise of the imagination."

Geranium reflexum

See *G. ×monacense*, page 78.

Geranium regelii

Height:	30 cm
Position:	Sun
Flower:	Pale blue or almost pure blue with purple veins. 4 cm
Season:	Early summer
Propagation:	Division, rhizomes, seed

Geranium regelii comes from the Himalayas and is often described as a miniature *G. pratense*. *Geranium regelii*, which was first used in gardens in the 1990s, is easy to grow. However, in my garden it sometimes skips over its flowering stage. As luck would have it, it has done so this year just when

G. renardii

G. renardii
'Tcschelda'

G. 'Chantilly'

G. 'Philippe Vapelle'

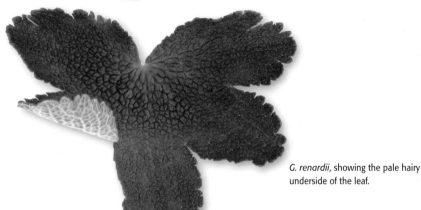

G. renardii, showing the pale hairy underside of the leaf.

I wanted a picture of its pretty pale blue flowers for my book. The species gets its name from the botanist E. Regel.

Geranium renardii

Height:	30 cm
Position:	Sun
Flower:	Whitish with purple veins, pale violet. 3.5–4 cm
Season:	Early summer
Propagation:	Division, seed (but the varieties are not true to seed)

Geranium renardii comes from the Caucasus. You can see by the leaves that the plant must have sun and well-drained soil, as they are thick with fine hairs—a structure that inhibits evaporation. The leaves are very attractive and grey-green in colour and thus not easily mistaken.

The petals of the flower do not sit close together but slightly apart, which makes the pale purple flowers very distinctive. The species was introduced by Walter Ingwersen (see page 73) in 1935. Use in rock gardens or at the front of beds. Flowers best in poor soil.

Above: *Geranium* 'Stephanie' (*G. renardii* × *G. peloponnesiacum*) is a very early blooming hybrid of *G. renardii*.

Varieties

G. renardii **'Tcschelda'**
Pale violet with purple veins. Discovered in the Caucasus by Dr. Hans Simon of Germany.

G. renardii **'Walter Ingwersen'**
Whitish with purple veins. This is the varietal name of geraniums sold as *G. renardii*.

G. renardii **'Zetterlund'**
Pale mauve with violet veins.

Other

Geranium renardii can be crossed with *G. platypetalum*. The hybrid was discovered in two locations in the wild and was first described in 1949. More recently, it has been cultivated with success by a Belgian, Ivan Louette, and Alan Bremner in the Orkney Islands. The Belgian hybrid was christened 'Philippe Vapelle'. As Bremner's plant is almost identical, this hybrid also bears the same name. And how lucky it is that the "child" has inherited the best features from each parent: the pretty foliage of *G. renardii* and the beautiful dark violet flowers of *G. platypetalum*.

'Chantilly' resembles a small pink renardii, and is the result of crossing *G. renardii* with *G. gracile*. *Geranium* 'Stephanie', which flowers very early in the year, is a cross between *G. renardii* and *G. peloponnesiacum*.

Geranium 'Terre Franche' is supposed to be an enhanced form of *G.* 'Philippe Vapelle', but is almost identical; in any case the flowers of both varieties are identical.

Geranium richardsonii

Height: 30–60 cm
Position: Sun
Flower: White (can also be pale pink), bluish purple stamens. 3 cm
Season: Early summer
Propagation: Division, seed

Geranium richardsonii is from western North America, where it grows in damp locations. The leaves are dark green, 5–10 cm across with a slight sheen and deep indentations. In gardens, the plant works well beside ponds. My own example of the species grows next to my little pond, but as this pond is artificial, the soil is quite dry. Therefore, I give the plant some compost to prevent the roots from drying out, and a little water may evaporate from the pond to help add moisture to the air around the plants. Obviously, the plant does not need a lot of moisture, as it is thriving and clearly feels at home. After all, it can see the water.

The species was named after Sir John Richardson, who was an explorer and naturalist.

G. richardsonii

Geranium ×riversleaianum

(*G. endressii* × *G. traversii*)
Height: 20 cm
Position: Sun
Flower: Pink, magenta. 3 cm
Season: Midsummer
Propagation: Division, no seeds produced

Geranium ×riversleaianum is the collective name for all *G. endressii* × *G. traversii* hybrids. As the two parent species grow in different parts of the world, southern Europe and New Zealand respectively, these hybrids have been developed in the garden. Unfortunately, these geraniums are not hardy in northern Europe and the United Kingdom.

Geranium ×riversleaianum has attractive leaves of a grey-green tone due to small hairs, which give them a silky look. The flowers sit on long creeping stems. Plant in full sun in a rock garden or at the front of a bed in well-drained soil, as these hybrids do not tolerate winter moisture well. To counteract this problem, you can plant

G. ×riversleaianum on sloping ground in the rock garden, so that moisture is not retained in the soil during the winter, but runs off. You can also try covering the plant during the winter to protect it from the cold and damp.

Varieties

G. ×riversleaianum '**Mavis Simpson**'
Pastel pink with pink veins and a white centre. The flowers have a silvery sheen, which looks beautiful next to its grey-green leaves. This variety was discovered as a seedling at the Royal Botanic Gardens, Kew, and was named after the employee who found it. (See photograph on page 13.)

G. ×riversleaianum '**Russell Prichard**'
Warm magenta-red with red veins. Named after a member of the family that owned the nursery where the variety originated (see "Other", below). This variety is less hardy than 'Mavis Simpson'.

Other

As the first hybrid of *G. endressii* and *G. traversii* originated at the Riverslea Nursery in Hampshire, England, Peter Yeo chose the collective name *G. ×riversleaianum* for these hybrids in 1985. The first hybrid was included under the name *G. traversii* 'Prichard's Hybrid' in Ingwersen's 1946 book on the *Geranium* genus (see page 122), in which he wrote that the hybrid came to his nursery from Prichard's nursery at Riverslea in Hampshire, and that it had unfortunately been lost during the war. This means that the hybrid must have existed before the Second World War.

Right: *Geranium robertianum* grows very wild and seeds itself freely. It is also called herb Robert.

Geranium rivulare

Height:	45 cm
Position:	Sun, partial shade
Flower:	White with violet veins and stamens. 1–2.5 cm
Season:	Early summer
Propagation:	Division, seed

Geranium rivulare (synonyms *G. aconitifolium*, *G. sylvaticum* subsp. *rivulare*) originates in the western and central areas of the Alps. The species name means "found near rivers and streams", which is a bit misleading. The plant does not require any special care in the garden.

Geranium rivulare is an erect plant with divided leaves caused by indentations reaching almost to the middle. It produces a large number of funnel-shaped white flowers.

Geranium robertianum

Height:	35 cm
Position:	Sun, shade, partial shade
Flower:	Pink, white. 1 cm
Season:	Entire summer
Propagation:	Seed—read on

Geranium robertianum is a biennial that grows wild in most of the United Kingdom, Europe, North Africa and North Asia. This species is widely known as herb Robert, but it is also called "stinking cranesbill", a name well chosen as the plant's long, downy hairs produce a strong scent. At first glance, it looks quite sweet. The leaves are delicately indented and the stems are reddish. Herb Robert's abundant small pink flowers are charming. Unfortunately, this species also produces abundant seed and the huge number of resultant seedlings creates a veritable plague. Never let *G. robertianum* into your garden. The species also occurs in a white-flowered version with the name *G. robertianum* 'Celtic White'. The white is also problematic, so it's really a case of choosing the lesser of two evils.

Other

As you have probably gathered, I have struggled considerably with *G. robertianum*. I have never been able to exterminate it, though it has been many years since I planted it in the garden. I got the plant from a friend, who had herself bought the seeds from Thompson & Morgan. I can at least confirm what the label on the seed packet said: "Wild Geraniums". *Geranium robertianum* is only included in this book so I can pass on this warning.

Perhaps I should take this opportunity to offer a warning about geraniums in general—they are quite addictive. After twenty years I'm still growing them, and my addiction is just getting worse.

Warning! Never introduce *G. robertianum* into your garden. The huge number of seedlings it produces is a veritable plague.

Right: *Geranium sanguineum* 'Shepherd's Warning', which is low-growing and a brilliant pink, and comes from Jack Drake in Scotland.

Geranium Rozanne

(*G. himalayense* × *G. wallichianum* 'Buxton's Variety')

Height:	40 cm
Position:	Sun, partial shade
Flower:	Deep blue with only a hint of red, whitish centre and black stamens. 4 cm
Season:	Entire summer
Propagation:	Particularly difficult, perhaps from stem cuttings

Geranium Rozanne ('Gerwat') was discovered in 1990 in the garden of Donald and Rozanne Waterer in Somerset, England. The plant proved very difficult to propagate. Attempts were made for many years before the plant was introduced at the 2000 Chelsea Flower Show in London by Blooms of Bressingham. The plants now available to buy have been micro-propagated (see page 13).

The plant is extremely vigorous and can put out stems that can grow to over a metre. It flowers for a very long time. Very similar to *G.* 'Jolly Bee' (see pages 43 and 67).

Geranium rubifolium

See *G. kishtvariense*, page 69.

Geranium ruprechtii

Height:	60 cm
Position:	Sun, partial shade
Flower:	Dark violet, violet stamens
Season:	Midsummer
Propagation:	Division, seed

Geranium ruprechtii is a little known geranium from Russia. It is reminiscent of *G. pratense*, although it flowers later and produces larger but fewer blooms.

Geranium 'Salome'

(*G. lambertii* × *G. procurrens*)
See *G. lambertii*, page 70.

Geranium sanguineum

Height:	15–50 cm
Position:	Sun
Flower:	White, pink, magenta, some with streaks. 3–4 cm
Season:	Midsummer
Propagation:	Division, rhizome, stem cuttings, seed (but not all varieties are true to seed)

Geranium sanguineum is native to Europe, the Caucasus and northern Turkey. Sanguineum comes from the Latin *sanguis*, which means blood. The plant is also called bloody cranesbill. In the past, it was grown for medicinal purposes and used as a healing salve, and the common name "bloody" probably refers to this rather than the colour of the flowers, which are not blood red at all.

In the wild this species is found in dry, sunny places and usually on chalky or limestone soils, scrub, dunes or cliffs and in granite areas. It is well-suited to the garden, even if the soil is neither alkaline nor contains granite. The leaves are small, kidney-shaped and very indented, forming slender lobes. You quickly learn to recognize the species by its foliage, but if you are in any doubt as to whether a geranium is a *sanguineum*, a sure sign is the solitary flowers. Other geraniums have flowers that bloom in pairs (see "Other", page 116). Plant it on the sunny side of the bed. The lowest-growing varieties work well in rock gardens. *Geranium sanguineum* forms quite dense clumps, but it takes a few years before the plant develops into something. On the other hand, once it takes hold, it is quite difficult to move, if you don't remove the new shoots that the rhizomes sends out. However, it is by no means a nuisance.

Geranium sanguineum and hybrids

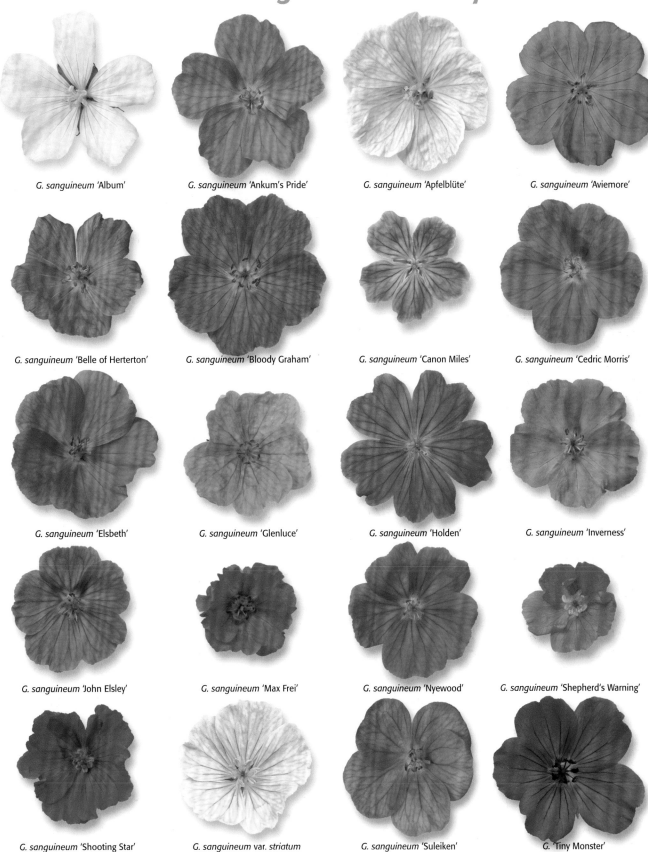

G. sanguineum 'Album'

G. sanguineum 'Ankum's Pride'

G. sanguineum 'Apfelblüte'

G. sanguineum 'Aviemore'

G. sanguineum 'Belle of Herterton'

G. sanguineum 'Bloody Graham'

G. sanguineum 'Canon Miles'

G. sanguineum 'Cedric Morris'

G. sanguineum 'Elsbeth'

G. sanguineum 'Glenluce'

G. sanguineum 'Holden'

G. sanguineum 'Inverness'

G. sanguineum 'John Elsley'

G. sanguineum 'Max Frei'

G. sanguineum 'Nyewood'

G. sanguineum 'Shepherd's Warning'

G. sanguineum 'Shooting Star'

G. sanguineum var. striatum

G. sanguineum 'Suleiken'

G. 'Tiny Monster'

G. sanguineum '**Jubilee Pink**'
20 cm. A very bright true pink. Very pretty geranium for use in rock gardens, but unfortunately it is not a vigorous grower.

G. sanguineum '**Little Bead**'
Low and compact. Magenta. It sometimes goes under the invalid name *G. sanguineum* 'Nanum'. There has been some confusion regarding names for low-growing *G. sanguineum*. *G. sanguineum* var. *prostratum*, which is a synonym of *G. sanguineum* var. *striatum*, is thus also used for low-growing varieties of *G. sanguineum* regardless of the colour of the flowers.

G. sanguineum '**Max Frei**'
20 cm. Magenta, mauve. Compact growth. Good autumn foliage colour.

G. sanguineum '**Nyewood**'
Extraordinarily similar to 'Max Frei', but of a slightly paler colour.

G. sanguineum '**Shepherd's Warning**'
25 cm. A lot like 'Jubilee Pink', but more vigorous and compact.

G. sanguineum '**Shooting Star**'
20 cm. Bright mauve with a pink sheen. A cross between 'Shepherd's Warning' and 'Elsbeth'.

G. sanguineum var. **striatum**
(synonym *G. sanguineum* var. *lancastrense*) 25 cm. Pale pink with deep pink streaks. A particularly beautiful plant, which reproduces itself consistently from seed. The synonym refers to Lancashire in northeast England (see "Other", below).

G. sanguineum var. **striatum** '**Splendens**'
A version in slightly darker shades of pink.

G. sanguineum '**Suleiken**'
30 cm. Magenta, pretty autumn foliage colour. Discovered in the wild by Dr. Hans Simon from Germany.

Varieties

G. sanguineum '**Album**'
40 cm. Large pure white flowers. According to Ingwersen, it was created in a garden in Scotland.

G. sanguineum '**Ankum's Pride**'
25 cm. Dark pink of a pure, bright hue. Long flowering. From Coen Jansen in Holland, who wanted to improve on 'Shepherd's Warning'.

G. sanguineum '**Apfelblüte**'
25 cm. Very pale pink. A particularly dainty geranium well-suited to rock gardens owing to its small stature.

G. sanguineum '**Aviemore**'
30 cm. Mauve.

G. sanguineum '**Belle of Herterton**'
25 cm. Compact. Pink and veined.

G. sanguineum '**Bloody Graham**'
20 cm. Magenta. Large flowers and creeping growth with long "swaying" stems. Discovered in the garden of Graham Stuart Thomas, eminent English horticulturist who died in 2003.

G. sanguineum '**Canon Miles**'
20 cm. Pink with pale centre. As the blooms age, they develop a narrow creamy white edge. Suitable for rock gardens owing to its small stature.

G. sanguineum '**Cedric Morris**'
50 cm. Bright magenta-red flowers, which are also very large. Found growing wild in Wales by English painter and gardener Cedric Morris.

G. sanguineum '**Droplet**'
Only a few inches high. Magenta. Believed to come true from seed. The invalid name *G. sanguineum* 'Minutum' has been used for this variety.

G. sanguineum '**Elsbeth**'
Similar to 'Cedric Morris', but this plant is hairier.

G. sanguineum '**Glenluce**'
30 cm. Pale mauve flowers. A variety discovered near the Scottish town of Glenluce in 1937 by A. T. Johnson.

G. sanguineum '**Holden**'
20 cm. Brilliant dark pink. Creeping growth.

G. sanguineum '**Inverness**'
15 cm. Pale mauve. Flat growth, which is why it is suitable for rock gardens.

G. sanguineum '**John Elsley**'
15 cm. Brilliant dark pink. Very flat growth. Good in a rock garden or at the front of a bed.

Other

Geranium sanguineum is in a class of its own, with a different number of chromosomes. Whereas geraniums generally have 28 chromosomes, *G. sanguineum* has 84, exactly three times the normal number.

Below: 1 *G. sanguineum* 'Canon Miles' is particularly well suited to rock gardens, as it is low-growing.
2 This is *G. sanguineum* 'Shooting Star', which is shown here growing between the lowest branches of a small shrub, *Sorbus chamaemespilus*.
3 *G. sanguineum* 'Apfelblüte'

Almost all cultivated geraniums have paired flowers, but *G. sanguineum* is an exception, as it has solitary flowers (*G. traversii*, *G. sessiliflorum* and *G. hayatanum* are among the very few other geraniums that have individual blooms).

When you sow seeds from a *G. sanguineum*, you can be reasonably certain of getting a *G. sanguineum*, as it is one of nature's oddities and its increased number of chromosomes means it does not cross with other geraniums. However, in the late 1980s, an English garden proved to be home to a seedling reckoned to be a cross between *G. sanguineum* and *G. wlassovianum*. It was given the name *G.* 'Khan'.

People have tried to cross *G. sanguineum* with other geranium species, but this has resulted in few successes. These include crossing *G. sanguineum* with *G. psilostemon*, which produced *G.* 'Little David' and *G.* 'Tiny Monster'.

You can see clearly from the foliage and flowers of a sanguineum hybrid that one parent was indeed a *G. sanguineum*. Peter Yeo (taxonomist at the University Botanic Garden, Cambridge), writes that this is probably due to the large number of chromosomes that *G. sanguineum* contributes, so hybrids inherit more genetic information from *G. sanguineum* than from the other parent. Other sanguineum hybrids include *G.* 'Diva' and *G.* 'Dilys'.

I always thought that the well-known and much-loved *G. sanguineum* var. *striatum* (synonym *G. sanguineum* var. *lancastrense*) had been discovered as a unique plant in the wild, in this case in Lancashire, England. I have recently read that this variant of *G. sanguineum* is spread throughout the area surrounding Barrow-in-Furness. This is the only place in the world where this plant grows wild (although the area was formerly part of Lancashire, it is now in Cumbria). Some botanists regard this variety as a species in itself, and this could also explain why it propagates consistently from seed. I also read at the same time that it is known that it was cultivated before 1732. A man ahead of his times, Dr. James Sherard (1666–1738) was growing the plant in his botanical garden in Eltham, now a suburb of London. This garden contained one of Europe's best collection of plants, and Sherard employed someone to write and illustrate a book—a catalogue—of the plants in the garden. The book, entitled *Hortus Elthamensis*, was published in 1732 and included *G. sanguineum* var. *lancastrense*.

A plant has appeared on the market under the name of *G. sanguineum* 'Plenum'. I contacted an English nursery that sells it to find out whether it really is a double *G. sanguineum*. Unfortunately, it is not. The flowers have a few extra petals, so it is no "rose". The nursery therefore missed out on my "send immediately" letter.

Geranium sessiliflorum subsp. *novaezelandiae*

Height:	3 cm
Position:	Sun
Flower:	Whitish. 1 cm
Season:	Midsummer
Propagation:	Seed

Geranium sessiliflorum subsp. *novaezelandiae* comes, as suggested by its name, from New Zealand. It is an interesting plant that really needs to be in a rock garden. The plant must be in soil that is easily permeated by winter rain, which these small alpine geraniums cannot tolerate (see the section entitled "Hardy Geraniums for Rock Gardens"). Its small whitish flowers grow singly (see also *G. sanguineum* "Other"). However, it is not for the flowers but for the brown or copper-coloured leaves that we grow this small cranesbill. It is slightly tricky to position the plant so that the leaf colour is not lost in the surrounding soil. I grow this particular cranesbill between or against light-coloured stones in the rock garden. Another option is to plant it alongside rock garden plants with pale or yellow variegated leaves, so they provide a contrast to the brown leaves. *Geranium sessiliflorum* subsp. *novaezelandiae* may not be completely hardy (it isn't in Denmark), but generally survives the harsh, wet winters through its numerous seedlings.

Varieties

G. sessiliflorum subsp. *novaezelandiae* 'Nigricans'
Whitish. Brown leaves.
G. sessiliflorum subsp. *novaezelandiae* 'Porter's Pass'
Whitish. Its leaves are reddish brown and glossy.

Other

G. sessiliflorum subsp. *novaezelandiae* has whitish flowers—of course, you might say, since it is from New Zealand. Over 60 percent of the plants pollinated by insects there have pale-coloured flowers. The islands' heather, harebells and gentians are also white. The explanation for this is that there are no indigenous bees in New Zealand (they do have them now, as they have been introduced), so the flowers are pollinated by flies and mosquitoes. Such insects are very attracted to pale colours, so in order to be noticed by pollinators, the flowers have to be pale.

Below: *Geranium sessiliflorum* subsp. *novaezelandiae* 'Nigricans' has very pale flowers, like many other plants from New Zealand.

Leaf: *G. sessiliflorum* subsp. *novaezelandiae* 'Porter's Pass'

The next question is why there were no bees originally in New Zealand. For the answer to that we have to go back a hundred million years, to a time before any flowering plants began developing specialized pollination mechanisms involving the help of the more highly developed insects. At that time New Zealand and Australia were joined to South America. Over sixty million years ago New Zealand broke away from South America and gradually drifted to its current location. And for one reason or another wildlife in this corner of the world has evolved differently from elsewhere. Consequently, no bees evolved in New Zealand, and the arrangement between flowers and bees, which I wrote about in the section entitled "Hardy Geraniums and Bees", never came into being there. Evolution also took a very different path in other areas of the plant and animal kingdom.

On board as New Zealand drifted away was *G. sessiliflorum*, leaving behind masses of relatives in South America, which remain there to this day. Australia also drifted away from South America carrying relatives of

G. sessiliflorum. In each of these three locations *G. sessiliflorum* has evolved slightly differently. Consequently, the species is divided into three subspecies: *G. sessiliflorum* subsp. *sessiliflorum* from South America, *G. sessiliflorum* subsp. *brevicaule* from Australia, and *G. sessiliflorum* subsp. *novaezelandiae*, as mentioned, from New Zealand.

So there is a whole history to reflect on when you see this little brown-leaved geranium in a rock garden. That's the best thing about it, in my opinion.

Geranium shikokianum

Height: 20–40 cm
Position: Partial shade, sun
Flower: Pink with a network of purple veins and a large white centre. 3 cm
Season: Midsummer
Propagation: Division, seed

Geranium shikokianum comes from Japan and Korea. It is a bushy plant that produces

Other

In the section on flowers and bees I mentioned that there are five nectaries in a geranium flower. However, there is always an exception to the rule and this is it. For *G. sinense* only has one nectary, which is positioned centrally, like a greenish ring with indents from which the petals radiate. According to Peter Yeo, it is also the only geranium with just one nectary. The nectar is very easily accessible in this ring, and the flower attracts a myriad insects, particularly hoverflies looking for a little "fast food".

Geranium 'Sirak'

(*G. gracile* × *G. ibericum*)
Height: 50 cm
Position: Sun, shade
Flower: Mauve, dark veins, pale eye.
               4–5 cm
Season: Midsummer
Propagation: Division

G. 'Sirak'

Geranium 'Sirak' comes from Hans Simon of Germany, and Alan Bremner; the two of them have to share the credit, as the hybrid originated simultaneously in both places. This plant resembles a "pink *G.* ×*magnificum*".

long stems. The leaves are deeply indented and attractively mottled, while their underside is smooth and glossy. This species cannot tolerate drying out, and is therefore best in a slightly shady location. It is supposed to be very easy to propagate either by division or sowing seed.

Varieties

G. shikokianum* var. *quelpaertense
Low-growing variety that is hairier than the other two. This variety is only found on Cheju Island between Japan and Korea.
G. shikokianum* var. *shikokianum
Looser growth than the other two varieties. Very attractive mottling on the leaves. Comes from the Japanese mainland.
G. shikokianum* var. *yoshiianum
A low-growing variety, up to 30 cm, with highly mottled foliage from the island of Yakushima, located in the far south of Japan. Introduced by Bleddyn and Sue Wynn-Jones, Crûg Farm Plants. (See also *G. koreanum* on page 69.)

Geranium sinense

Height: 60 cm
Position: Partial shade, shade
Flower: Dark red, reflexed petals are
               reddish at the base, and red
               stamens. 2 cm
Season: Midsummer
Propagation: Division, seed

Geranium sinense gets its name from its country of origin, China; *sinense* means "resident of Sina"; Sina is the Latin name for China. This species has most unusual dark flowers that "bow their heads and sweep their petals back". The leaves are indented, dark green and slightly glossy. *Geranium sinense* grows slowly, and I feel it is difficult to position so you can see the distinctive flowers. You need to plant it in a raised position in a woodland bed or border, so it is clearly visible.

Right: *Geranium* 'Spinners' has dark, royal blue cup-shaped flowers.

Geranium soboliferum

Height:	30–40 cm
Position:	Partial shade (can tolerate sun if the soil is very moist)
Flower:	Deep pink with dark veins. 3–4.5 cm
Season:	Late summer
Propagation:	Division, seed (the varieties are not true to seed)

G. soboliferum 'Starman'

Geranium soboliferum grows wild in Manchuria, Japan and Siberia, in the area around Ussuri. This species is not easy to accommodate in gardens, as it requires very damp soil. The leaves are highly indented and resemble enlarged versions of those of *G. sanguineum*. Fortunately, the varieties of *G. soboliferum* are easier to grow. Nurseryman Rolf Offenthal has worked on this species and provisionally created two varieties, only one of which is available for sale. The other is expected to come on the market around 2006. Both varieties are winter-hardy and easy to divide.

Varieties

G. soboliferum 'Alien's Gift'

30–40 cm. Very deep pink with magenta veins. The veins are strongly coloured. Around the centre of the flower the colour runs out, so the bloom is clearly divided into a pale outer section and a dark inner section, which forms a distinct cinquefoil. Seedling from 'Starman'. Not yet on sale.

G. soboliferum 'Starman'

40 cm. Very deep pink with magenta veins. The flower is approximately 4.5 cm across. The veins are strongly coloured. The outer section of the petals is clearly paler than the dark central section, which forms a fine star. This two-tone flower immediately steals the scene, so the name is well chosen.

Other

Rolf Offenthal sowed a large quantity of seeds from *G. soboliferum*. From among the hundreds of seedlings, he selected one with a very distinctly two-tone flower and a good compact stature. The selected seedling, which was given the name 'Starman', flowers from mid July to the end of September (from mid-summer well into autumn). In this respect, it is also an improvement on *G. soboliferum*, which finishes flowering by September. The new variety, 'Alien's Gift', which is in the pipeline, has an even longer flowering season, beginning flowering at the end of June.

Geranium soboliferum belongs to a group of geraniums called the "Krameri Group" by Peter Yeo. These all come from the Far East and resemble one another. The group consists of: *G. dahuricum*, *G. hayatanum*, *G. krameri*, *G. soboliferum* and *G. yesoense*. *G. soboliferum* is often incorrectly sold as *G. yesoense* var. *nipponicum*.

Geranium 'Spinners'

(*G. pratense* × *G.* ?)

Height:	90 cm
Position:	Sun
Flower:	Bluish purple, almost royal blue. 3 cm
Season:	Early summer
Propagation:	Division, basal cuttings

Geranium 'Spinners' is an elegant plant with cup-shaped, dark blue flowers and attractive, highly indented leaves. Only one of the parents of this hybrid is known: *G. pratense*, which fortunately only seems to have passed on its best characteristics to *G.* 'Spinners'. In particular, I have never seen one with mildew, which can plague *G. pratense*.

121

Right: Geranium 'Sue Crûg'

Below: Geranium 'Stephanie'

Other

The story of *G.* 'Spinners' begins in Seattle, U.S.A. Marvin Black was a parks department gardener there, and he sent seeds from *G. pratense* to the Spinners Nursery in Hampshire, England. Among the resulting seedlings, the owner of Spinners discovered one that was different. This plant initially circulated under various incorrect names such as *G. bergianum*, *G. pratense* 'Kashmir Purple' and *G. clarkei* 'Kashmir Purple'; it was finally introduced in 1990 under the name *G.* 'Spinners' by Axletree Nursery.

Geranium 'Stephanie'

(*G. peloponnesiacum* × *G. renardii* ?)

Height:	35 cm
Position:	Sun
Flower:	Pale violet with very distinct dark purple veins
Season:	Early summer
Propagation:	Division

Geranium 'Stephanie', which is thought to be a hybrid of *G. peloponnesiacum* and *G. renardii*, has both very pretty flowers and attractive foliage. The latter are probably inherited from *G. renardii*, whose leaves were appropriately described by writer Will Ingwersen (see "Other", below) as "reptilian". It is the delightful honeycomb look of these grey-green leaves that he was referring to. The thick leaves and the hairs on them are the plant's protection against excessive water loss, equipping it for sun and drought. *G.* 'Stephanie' is therefore suitable for rock gardens, but can also be positioned at the front of a sunny herbaceous border.

Other

Will Ingwersen, who was the son of nurseryman Walter Ingwersen (see page 73), began his writing activities due to a shortage of paper. This shortage was due to the

Second World War, which caused paper to be strictly rationed. Consequently, paper could not be obtained for commercial purposes such as catalogues, but was available for educational works. Therefore father and son hit upon the idea of printing their catalogue as small brochures, each dealing with an individual genus.

One of these covered the *Geranium* genus, and Peter Yeo refers to it in his book. It is, in actual fact, from this brochure that he knows that Walter Ingwersen introduced *G. renardii* in 1935. Will Ingwersen went on to write more substantial works, including the *Manual of Alpine Plants* (1978). I myself have a little book, *Dianthus* from 1949, by Walter and dedicated to his father, with whom he got on particularly well. Incidentally, it was his father who originally taught Will to read and write; Walter Ingwersen deeply distrusted the school system and opted to teach his son himself.

Geranium 'Sue Crûg'

(*G. ×oxonianum* × *G.* 'Salome')

Height:	40 cm
Position:	Sun
Flower:	Reddish violet with dark purple veins and blackish purple centre, black stamens. 4 cm
Season:	Midsummer
Propagation:	Division

Geranium 'Sue Crûg' comes from the Crûg Farm nursery in Wales (Crûg is pronounced "kriig"). There are actually four geraniums "intermixed" in this hybrid, as it is a cross of two crosses. Unfortunately one of its parents (*G.* 'Salome') has two non-hardy parents, so that is why *G.* 'Sue Crûg' may not prove totally hardy. This is frustrating, as the hybrid has very pretty, somewhat dramatic flowers of black and violet. *G.* 'Sue Crûg' is a broad, low-growing plant, with foliage reminiscent of that of *G. ×oxonianum*.

Geranium Summer Skies

(*G. himalayense* 'Plenum' × *G. pratense*)

Height:	60 cm
Position:	Sun
Flower:	Lavender with a hint of pink, dark veins
Season:	Midsummer
Propagation:	Division, basal cuttings

Geranium **Summer Skies** (*G.* 'Gernic') is a hybrid that resembles *G. pratense*. It has double flowers and greyish green foliage. It was created by Kevin Nicholson and introduced by Blooms of Bressingham. It is a demanding plant, so give it plenty of water and compost.

Right, above and below: *Geranium* **Summer Skies** is one of the few geraniums that requires regular feeding.

Geranium sylvaticum and hybrids

G. sylvaticum 'Amy Doncaster'   G. sylvaticum 'Angulatum'   G. sylvaticum 'Baker's Pink'   G. sylvaticum 'Birch Lilac'

G. sylvaticum 'Ice Blue'   G. sylvaticum 'Immaculée'   G. sylvaticum 'Lilac Time'   G. sylvaticum 'Nikita'

G. sylvaticum 'Silva'   G. 'Mary Mottram'   G. 'Prelude'

Geranium sylvaticum

Height:	40–130 cm
Position:	Partial shade, sun
Flower:	Blue, violet, purple, pale pink, white. 2–3 cm
Season:	Early summer and often again after cutting back
Propagation:	Division, basal cuttings, seed (varieties do not all come true from seed)

Left, above: G. sylvaticum 'Immaculée' often flowers again later in the summer.
Below: G. sylvaticum flourishes in woodland.

Geranium sylvaticum, (can also be seen written "silvaticum") originates from Europe and northern Turkey.

The species name means "grows in woodland", and in the wild you find it in damp, fertile humus-rich soil in woodland or meadows.

The flowers are generally violet with a small white eye, but you can also find plants with white and pink flowers. In northeastern Europe, for some reason, the white and pink varieties are more common the further north you go.

In the garden, in addition to varieties in the colours mentioned, we also have an extremely pretty pure blue variety that originated in a garden. Geranium sylvaticum has large leaves; its leaf is generally like a hand with seven fingers. This is a characteristic you can use to distinguish this species from G. pratense, which has highly indented leaves with numerous fingers. Geranium sylvaticum flowers early and looks attractive combined with other plants that flower in the early summer, such as epimediums, primulas, Siberian bugloss (Brunnera) and bulbous plants. The white varieties of G. sylvaticum are excellent together with bleeding heart (Dicentra spectabilis). The perennials mentioned also thrive, like G. sylvaticum, in slightly shady spots.

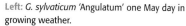

Left: *G. sylvaticum* 'Angulatum' one May day in growing weather.
Below left: *G. sylvaticum* 'Amy Doncaster' is almost pure blue.
Below: *G. sylvaticum* 'Immaculée' is a low-growing variety.

Geranium sylvaticum can also tolerate sun, provided the soil is not dry, which can easily happen when the sun is beating down in summer. Therefore all my varieties of *G. sylvaticum* are in shady beds. To give the bed fertile topsoil, I mulch the soil around the plants with compost.

Varieties

Unless otherwise indicated, the height is approximately 70 cm.

G. sylvaticum f. *albiflorum*
White. Found growing in the wild.

G. sylvaticum 'Album'
White. Lacks the pigment anthocyanin and is therefore an albino. Comes true from seed.

G. sylvaticum 'Amy Doncaster'
Pure blue with a white centre. Exceptionally beautiful.

G. sylvaticum 'Angulatum'
90 cm. Pale pink with veins. Very large flowers. The name 'Angulatum' is related to the word "angle" and alludes to the twisted stems, but you have to look hard to see the twist—the plant is not crooked.

G. sylvaticum 'Baker's Pink'
(formerly known as *G.* 'Wengen')
130 cm. Pale pink. Large flowers.

Discovered in the Swiss Alps by Bill Baker (see page 94). Flowers slightly later than the other varieties, but for much longer.

G. sylvaticum 'Birch Lilac'
Violet. May be confused with 'Mayflower'. However, its white eye is larger.

G. sylvaticum 'Ice Blue'
Very pale violet. Beautiful variety from Coen Jansen in Holland.

G. sylvaticum 'Immaculée'
50 cm. Pure white. Large flowers. This plant is very vigorous, and some years it flowers again later in the season. From Coen Jansen.

G. sylvaticum 'Lilac Time'
40 cm. Magenta. Small flowers. From Coen Jansen.

G. sylvaticum 'Mayflower'
Violet with white eye. An enhanced version of the species. Introduced around 1972 by Alan Bloom, of the Blooms of Bressingham nursery.

G. sylvaticum 'Nikita'
50 cm. Beautiful pure blue flower with white centre. A seedling that originated in the garden of Daniel Hinkley, Heronswood Nursery, U.S.A. In his book *The Explorer's Garden* (1999), Hinkley explains that visitors passing the plant stopped short to admire its beautiful blue flowers. As the plant was close to the spot where Hinkley's cocker spaniel was buried, he decided it would be fitting to name the seedling in memory of his dog 'Nikita'.

G. sylvaticum 'Silva'
Reddish violet. From Ernst Pagel in northern Germany.

G. sylvaticum var. wanneri
40 cm. Pale pink with veins. Low-growing plant that is less vigorous than the preceding varieties.

Other

It is a familiar story: the flower colour is described as blue, and yet the plant has violet or purplish blue flowers. Very few plants have flowers that are truly blue. *Geranium sylvaticum* 'Amy Doncaster' is one

such rarity; it has pure deep blue colouring and is extremely close to being true blue. This variety originated in the garden of a very keen gardener, after whom the plant is named. She lived in Chandler's Ford, Hampshire, England, and had a very large garden well populated with woodland plants.

Amy Doncaster lived to over a hundred—I am tempted to say "Of course!". You see, gardeners frequently live to a ripe old age. We have to, since it seems that people generally do not discover the delights of gardening until middle age.

I wrote a series of articles in *Haven* (2002 and 2003) entitled "Significant gardeners", about well-known individuals whose names are linked to garden plants. Many of the celebrities didn't begin their mission in life until they were over fifty, but on the other hand they lived a long time. It was a very heartening topic to work on.

There are a few hybrids with *G. sylvaticum* as one of the parents. In my garden I have a fairly new one, *G.* 'Red Admiral', which is a cross of *G. sylvaticum* 'Baker's Pink' and *G. psilostemon*. (See page 110.)

Geranium thunbergii

Height:	25 cm
Position:	Sun, shade
Flower:	Varies from white to magenta with purple veins. 1.5 cm
Season:	Late summer
Propagation:	Seed. Sometimes the stems take root and produce new plants

Geranium thunbergii, which takes its name from Swedish botanist C. P. Thunberg, comes from northern China, Taiwan and Japan. This plant is hairy and rather weed-like, but as it can tolerate drought and shade, it can be used as ground cover in such awkward spots in the garden. Otherwise it is better suited to wild gardens.

Geranium thunbergii produces long trailing stems that take root here and there. It has pale green leaves that are deeply indented into five lobes and are 5–10 cm wide. At the base of the indentations there is almost always a pronounced reddish brown mark.

The species is closely related to *G. nepalense* and has been regarded as a variety of this. The latter species comes from Afghanistan, the Himalayas and China.

Geranium thunbergii can be distinguished from *G. nepalense* by the fact that the latter does not have the reddish brown marks at the base of the leaf indentations. *Geranium nepalense* has small, dark green, slightly mottled leaves that are often reddish on the underside and brownish on the upper side. This species is, however, just as weed-like as *G. thunbergii*.

Another species *G. thunbergii* is very often confused with is *G. yoshinoi* from Japan, a 60-cm tall, erect plant with white or pale pink flowers with dark veins. The two species flower at about the same time. Packets of seeds that are supposed to be of *G. yoshinoi* often turn out to contain seeds of *G. thunbergii* instead. Consequently, many of the plants sold as *G. yoshinoi* are in actual fact *G. thunbergii*.

Varieties

G. thunbergii 'Jester's Jacket'

Pale pink. A seed strain with leaves that are attractively covered with cream and pink-coloured patches. The catalogue from Plant World Botanic Garden, in Devon, England, states: "This attractively variegated form of *Geranium thunbergii* really is the first true-to-seed variegated hardy geranium."

I don't know how this variety behaves in gardens, or whether it seeds itself wildly. Since, as mentioned above, *G. thunbergii* and *G. yoshinoi* are often confused, you might be tempted to suppose that any plant sold under the name *G. yoshinoi* 'Confetti' is in fact *G. thunbergii* 'Jester's Jacket'.

Above: *G. thunbergii* 'Jester's Jacket'

Right: *Geranium* 'Tiny Monster' flowers profusely over a long period.

Geranium 'Tiny Monster'

(*G. sanguineum* × *G. psilostemon*)

Height: Up to 40 cm, but flat growth
Position: Sun
Flower: Magenta with very dark veins. 4 cm
Season: Entire summer
Propagation: Division, rhizomes

Geranium 'Tiny Monster' is a cross between two geranium species. The leaves and flowers show clear characteristics of one parent, *G. sanguineum*, while from the other parent, *G. psilostemon*, *G.* 'Tiny Monster' has inherited the dark tone to the colour of its flowers and its dark veins.

Geranium 'Tiny Monster' is an extremely vigorous plant that grows rapidly, exhibiting delightful dense growth. It is a little difficult to define the height of the plant, as it can easily shoot up individual stems around half a metre high. These rise up from the dense flat clump. *Geranium* 'Tiny Monster' is ideal at the front of a bed or in a rock garden. I have it growing below a rock garden in my garden, forming a border between the rock garden and the lawn. The plinths of the rock garden, the large rocks I use to keep the soil in the "mountain" are a necessary evil and can easily resemble a row of teeth, but *G.* 'Tiny Monster' hides the gaps between the "teeth" and prevents the rock garden looking like a set of dentures.

Geranium 'Tiny Monster' displays an amazing profusion of blooms over a very long period.

Other

As mentioned earlier, *G. sanguineum* has generally proved very difficult to cross with other *Geranium* species. However, German nurseryman Rolf Offenthal has managed to successfully cross the species with *G. psilostemon*, and the plant came on the market in the late 1990s.

When we have held Open Garden events I have been asked by numerous visitors why this geranium is called 'Tiny Monster'—was there something monstrous about it? I put this question to Rolf Offenthal, who explained that when he saw how rapidly the little seedling grew from almost nothing into a small bush, it made him think of a monster.

Evidently the visitors to my garden are not the only ones who are slightly dubious about this, as the name of the hybrid has had to be changed in order to sell to the American market. A witty colleague of Rolf Offenthal's launched the plant for him in America under the name *G.* '**Rolf Royce**'. An excellent name, as a garden is certainly well off with this hybrid in its beds.

Geranium traversii

Height: 20 cm
Position: Sun
Flower: White, pale pink with lighter borders. 2.5–3 cm
Season: Midsummer
Propagation: Seed, basal cuttings

Geranium traversii is indigenous to the Chatham Islands, 640 km east of New Zealand. Just think, geraniums grow there too; so the genus has certainly done well.

This little geranium has dark green leaves, 5–10 cm across, that are deeply indented into seven lobes, and greyish hairs that give the plant a silvery sheen. The flowers are, of course, pale, as the plant is from the New Zealand region (see "Other" under *G. sessiliflorum*, page 119). This species is one of a small group of geraniums with solitary rather than paired flowers.

Geranium traversii is an alpine plant for the rock garden. It is not hardy in the United Kingdom.

Geranium traversii also comes in a variety with pale pink flowers, *G. traversii* var. *elegans*, which is often one of the parents of the numerous hybrids between *G. traversii* and *G. sessiliflorum*.

It has been decided that crosses between *G. traversii* and *G. sessiliflorum* should have the collective name *G. ×antipodeum*.

It has likewise been decided that crosses between *G. traversii* and *G. endressii* should be known as *G. ×riversleaianum*.

Geranium traversii takes its name from ornithologist W. T. L. Travers.

Geranium tuberosum

Height: 25 cm
Position: Sun
Flower: Mauve with dark veins.
               2–3 cm
Season: Early summer
Propagation: Tubers, seed

Geranium tuberosum comes from the regions around the Mediterranean and further eastwards to Iran. The species name refers to the tubers. Tubers are the plant's food supply, enabling it to send out leaves and flowers in a hurry when the brief spring season with favourable growing conditions arrives.

After flowering, the plant dies down and only wakes again from dormancy the following spring, when the delicate, rather fern-like leaves come up again. *Geranium tuberosum* is suited to rock gardens, but can also be planted in beds in well-drained soil.

In its natural habitat this species is a common weed of cornfields and vineyards. The European variety belongs to the subspecies tuberosum. Consequently, it is called *G. tuberosum* subsp. *tuberosum*, while the Asian *G. tuberosum* is called *G. tuberosum* subsp. *linearifolium* Davis (synonym *G. stepporum* Davis). The two subspecies have slightly different leaves.

Geranium versicolor

Height: 40 cm
Position: Sun, partial shade
Colour: White, white with a network

Geranium versicolor has dark patches at the base of the leaf indentations.

of purple veins. The flowers are funnel-shaped
Flowers: Entire summer
Propagation: Division, basal cuttings, seed (but hybridizes freely with *G. endressii*)

Geranium versicolor (synonym *G. striatum*) comes from Italy, Greece and the former Yugoslavia. The foliage forms dense tufts, and the leaves are deeply indented and have a reddish brown spot at the base of each incision. The foliage is bright green in winter. I myself have never grown this species, but I have a number of its many "children" with *G. endressii* (the offspring are called *G. ×oxonianum*). Its roots are quite compact.

Varieties

G. versicolor 'Snow White'.
White with no coloured veins.

Geranium viscosissimum

Height: 70 cm
Position: Sun, partial shade
Flower: Pale pink or deep pink, dark veins and often with a white centre. 4 cm
Season: Early summer and again later
Propagation: Seed, basal cuttings. Tree-like roots, not suitable for dividing

Geranium viscosissimum comes from North America. The species name means "sticky", and there are sticky hairs on the stems. The leaves are deeply indented. It is a very pretty plant with large, flat flowers. Plant hunter Bill Baker (see page 94) tells how he found *G. viscossisimum* growing in a hot, dry spot where mugwort was growing in abundance. He also explains that as his own garden was cold and damp, plants of this species did not survive there long.

G. wallichianum 'Roze Tinten'

Geranium wallichianum

Height: 35 cm
Position: Partial shade
Flower: Blue, magenta, pink, many with a white centre and dark veins. 3 cm
Season: Late summer
Propagation: Extremely difficult to divide; seed, stem cuttings

Geranium wallichianum comes from the regions around the Himalayas. It forms a relatively low, creeping plant with lightly mottled and lobed leaves. The stipules, which are the small "flaps" located where the leaf stalk branches off from the main stem, are particularly large and round in this species. These stipules can be a distinguishing characteristic when the plant is not in bloom.

The colours of the flowers vary greatly from plant to plant in the wild. The flowers on one plant are uniform, but in a colony, twenty different variations can easily be present.

Geranium wallichianum is suitable for any section of rock garden that is not in full

Left: A distinguishing feature of *G. wallichianum* is the large round stipules, or "flaps", located where the leaf stalk branches off from the stem.
Below: *G. wallichianum* 'Buxton's Variety'

sunlight; the soil must not be too dry. It can also be grown in the lightest section of a woodland bed and under free-standing shrubs and trees.

Geranium wallichianum comes up in late spring. It doesn't make its entrance as a tight green tuft like most other geraniums however; it has shoots instead, and these stems can be used for cuttings (see page 39). Cut the stems into sections. Each section should have a few leaves. Pot the sections so the point where the leaves branch off from the stem is just above the compost. Place the cuttings in shade at first and keep the pots moist, but not sopping wet.

Some sources state that *G. wallichianum* should be covered in winter. I have now had this plant for several years without covering it in winter, although covering can't do it any harm. When protecting plants in winter, it is essential that the material used for covering is lightweight, as plants can easily rot if they remain under a wet cover all winter. Consequently, moisture-retaining mulches are not suitable.

The best-known variety is 'Buxton's Variety', also known as 'Buxton's Blue'.

Varieties

G. wallichianum 'Buxton's Variety'
(synonym 'Buxton's Blue')
Sky blue with a white centre, black stamens and dark veins. If it is warm, the flower is mauve; the colour changes to blue when the weather is colder. This variety is almost true to seed.

G. wallichianum 'Roze Tinten'
Dark mauve, white centre. This red version of the preceding variety is, unfortunately, not quite as true from seed as 'Buxton's Variety'. Therefore you should not expect a plant purchased with the name 'Roze Tinten' to have exactly the same flower as shown here in this book.

G. wallichianum 'Syabru'
Brilliant magenta with dark veins, without a white centre. The leaves are slightly downy

and are mottled with lime green. This variety is named after the village in Nepal where it was discovered.

Other

Geranium wallichianum 'Buxton's Variety' is obliging enough to be very close to coming true from seed, even though it is a variety. Only the best blues are selected to bear the name 'Buxton's Variety'. The variety is named after E. C. Buxton (1838–1925), who lived in the Conway valley in the far north of Wales. He had this extraordinarily beautiful variety of *G. wallichianum* in around 1920. I was astonished to read that this species is named after a Dane, Nathaniel Wallich, who was a surgeon and naturalist, and curator of Calcutta's botanical gardens. Calcutta was the capital of British India (1774–1912). Although the article I read by Jennifer Harmer in the Hardy Plant Society's magazine (Spring, 1999) gives no clear explanation of how he ended up there, it does say that Wallich was a very kind man who supported and encouraged the often slightly naive plant hunters sent out by high-ranking English patrons. *Geranium wallichianum* was introduced in 1820.

G. wlassovianum

Geranium wlassovianum

Height:	35 cm
Position:	Sun or partial shade
Flower:	Dark bluish purple with small white eye. 3–4 cm
Season:	Midsummer
Propagation:	Division, seed

Geranium wlassovianum comes from eastern Siberia, Mongolia and China. The foliage, which is velvety, is quite copper-coloured when it appears in the spring. It subsequently turns dark green, but the leaves retain a slightly copper tinge, and as the flowers are deep purplish blue, this geranium has a rather dark tone. You can take advantage of this by using this plant as a contrast to others with pale-coloured flowers. In autumn the foliage changes colour again, this time to red.

In the wild *G. wlassovianum* grows in slightly damp spots, but the species has adapted to life in gardens, and can hold its own even in fairly dry locations. It is a pity this geranium is not better known. I hope that this book will remedy that.

Varieties

G. wlassovianum 'Blue Star'
Dark bluish purple. The *G. wlassovianum* that has been in circulation in German nurseries has now been given this name.

G. wlassovianum 'Zellertal'
Dark purplish blue, distinguishable from the preceding variety by its very large flowers, approx. 4 cm.

Other

Geranium wlassovianum very rarely crosses with other species of the *Geranium* genus. This is probably because its chromosome count is 56, double the usual 28. However, it is thought to be one of the parents of the hybrid *G.* 'Khan'.

Geranium 'Lakwijk Star', which is soon due on the market, is considered by Coen Jansen to be a hybrid of *G. wlassovianum* (see "A visit to Coen Jansen", page 40).

Geranium yoshinoi

See page 128.

Below: *Geranium wlassovianum* displays beautiful colours as autumn approaches.

Other Geraniums

This list contains very brief descriptions of some of the rarer species and hybrids of the *Geranium* genus. There is very little literature available on these geraniums, so growing them is a matter of trial and error. Many of those listed have very little garden value, and so are really only for collectors.

Some of the species are annuals. The good thing about these is that you don't have to take them so seriously; there is no need to worry about them surviving the winter, because, of course, they don't.

Many of the hybrids that are not reliably hardy are also listed, for example the *G. traversii* hybrids.

G. antrorsum Alpine plant from Australia. 20 cm. Pink flowers.

G. 'Aya' *G. procurrens* × *G. traversii*. Mauve with dark eye.

G. bicknellii Annual from North America and Canada. 15–45 cm. Pink with dark veins.

G. biuncinatum Annual from Africa and Arabia. Brilliant dark pink.

G. 'Black Ice' *G. sessiliflorum* × *G. traversii*. Dark bronze-coloured foliage, almost black. White or pale pink.

G. brutium Annual from southern Italy, the Balkans and Turkey. 30 cm. Brilliant pink with blue-black stamens.

G. brycei From South Africa. Bushy plant. Bluish purple with white eye.

G. caeruleatum 25 cm. Considered by some to be a subspecies of *G. sylvaticum*. From the Balkans. Spreads rapidly by means of rhizomes. Small bluish white flowers.

G. caffrum Bushy and very leafy geranium from South Africa. White or pink.

G. canariense From the Canary Islands. 60 cm tall with large glossy, fragrant leaves. Dark pink.

G. carolinianum Annual from North America, Canada and Mexico. 35 cm. White or pale pink.

G. christensenianum Plant with long climbing stems. From China. Named after a Danish fern specialist. Autumn flowering.

White with purple veins. Difficult to grow.

G. 'Coombland White' *G. lambertii* × *G. traversii*. Mottled leaves. White or pale pink.

G. 'Crûg's Dark Delight' *G. sessiliflorum* × *G. traversii*. Very dark leaves. Pink.

G. dahuricum 45 cm. Trailing plant. From Asia, Russia and China. Pale pink with delicate red veins.

G. 'Derrick Cook' Unknown where this belongs in the genus. Yeo believes that it is a variety of *G. himalayense*. Others regard it as a separate species, as it is true to seed. Large white flowers (5 cm) with purple veins. Large indented leaves and reddish stems. Easy to divide by rhizomes. So new that for the time being only one nursery (Cranesbill Nursery, England) has it on sale according to *RHS Plant Finder* 2003–2004.

G. 'Elizabeth Ross' (*G. sessiliflorum* × *G. traversii*) × *G.* ×*oxonianum*. Small plant that is supposed to be the geranium with the reddest flowers.

G. favosum Annual from Africa. 25 cm. Brilliant pink with black eye.

G. 'Foie Gras' *G. sessiliflorum* × *G. traversii*. Reddish brown leaves. Pale pink.

G. fremontii 30–45 cm. From the west of North America. Large flowers (4 cm) over a long period, but the plant is inelegant in shape. Pale to dark pink.

G. glaberrimum Alpine plant from Turkey. 25 cm. Brilliant pink with red stamens. Best for an alpine house.

G. harveyi A rock garden geranium from South Africa. Magenta or bluish purple.

G. hayatanum From Taiwan (endemic, the only place where it grows wild). Half-metre-long, red climbing stems. Kidney-shaped, 6 cm broad leaves. The flowers (3 cm) grow singly. Pale mauve. Introduced a few years ago by Crûg Farm Plants.

G. hungaricum Some people may have searched for this species in the book without success. Since, to the best of my knowledge, this species does not exist, I have not included it as a main entry. The only information I could find about the

name *hungaricum* was in a German book (*Die Freiland-Schmuckstauden*, 2002, Ulmer), where the authors divide *G. phaeum* into three groups *phaeum* var. *lividum*, *phaeum* var. *phaeum* and *phaeum* var. *hungaricum*. Peter Yeo, however, only works with varieties *lividum* and *phaeum*.

G. incanum A rock garden geranium from South Africa. Very delicate, rather fern-like foliage. White, violet to magenta with dark veins.

G. 'Kate' *G. endressii* × *G. sessiliflorum* subsp. *novaezelandiae* 'Nigricans'. Small, short-lived plant with bronze-coloured foliage. Pale pink with dark veins.

G. kerberi Up to 100 cm. From Mexico and not hardy. White or lilac with bold dark veins.

G. kotschyi subsp. *charlesii* Tuberous plant. From Iran. Dark pink.

G. krameri Up to 80 cm, but quick to collapse. From China, Korea and Japan. Pale pink with darker veins.

G. linearilobum subsp. *transversale* Tuberous plant from Asia. Pink.

G. lucidum Annual. 30 cm. From Europe, Africa and China. Red stems and succulent, glossy leaves. Small flowers (1 cm). Pink. Frequently reseeds itself.

G. mascatense Annual. 30 cm. From Africa. Brilliant pink with a black eye.

G. moupinense From China. 35 cm. Deeply indented leaves. Large flowers (4 cm) in June. Lilac.

G. nanum Alpine plant, best suited to an alpine house. From the Atlas Mountains in Morocco. Pale pink or white with fine dark purple veins.

G. 'Nora Bremner' *G. rubifolium* × *G. wallichianum* 'Buxton's Variety'. 25 cm. Same stature as *G. wallichianum* 'Buxton's Variety'. Large star-shaped flower (4 cm), violet with white centre. Very difficult to propagate and problematic overall.

G. ocellatum Annual. From Africa, Arabia, the Himalayas and China. Small flower, mauve with black eye. The flowers often remain closed.

Right: *G. biuncinatum*, an annual from Africa and Arabia. (Photograph: Kirsten Lyng)
Below left: *G. canariense*.
Below right: *G. nanum*, an alpine plant from the Atlas Mountains, North Africa.
(Photograph: Kirsten Lyng)

G. 'Pink Spice' *G. sessiliflorum × G. traversii*. Burgundy leaves that turn dark green in cooler weather. Pink.

G. polyanthes 20–45 cm. Short-lived, according to Joy Jones and Trevor Bath. From the Himalayas and western China. Small kidney-shaped, succulent leaves. Brilliant pink.

G. potentilloides From Australia and New Zealand. Sporadic, small white or pink flowers on slender stems.

G. pseudosibiricum (Synonym *G. sylvaticum* subsp. *pseudosibiricum*) 40 cm. From the Ural Mountains and Siberia; resembles *G. rivulare*. Violet. Dioecious. Female flowers 1.5 cm; male flowers 2.5 cm.

G. pulchrum Up to 120 cm. From South Africa. Dark pink.

G. rectum From central Asia. Loose growth with scattered flowers. Brilliant pink with white centre and dark purple veins.

G. refractoides Synonym for *G. refractum*.

G. refractum 60 cm. From the Himalayas, Burma and China. Top section of the plant is covered with magenta hairs. Reflexed petals. White or pink to magenta.

G. robustum From South Africa. Large trailing plant. Bluish purple with white centre.

G. rubescens 60–90 cm. Biennial. From Madeira. Brilliant pink with magenta eye.

G. schiedeanum (Synonym *G. purpusii*) From Mexico. Low trailing plant. Lavender.

G. 'Sea Spray' *G. sessiliflorum × G. traversii*. Brownish-green leaves. White or pale pink.

G. sibiricum Trailing plant. From eastern Europe, China, Japan and the Himalayas. Small flowers (1 cm). White or pale pink with dark veins.

G. 'Stanhoe' *G. sessiliflorum × G. traversii*. Very compact plant. Green leaves. Pale pink.

G. stapfianum 15 cm. Plant for a rock garden or alpine house. From China and Tibet. Large flowers (4 cm). Dark magenta with dark veins.

G. subulato-stipulatum What a splendid name! From North America and Mexico. The plant has long stems, up to 80 cm and small flowers (1.5 cm). Magenta or dark purple with veins.

G. suzukii Small carpeting plant from Taiwan, where it is endemic (the only place where it grows wild). White. Introduced by Crûg Farm Plants.

G. swatense Low, hairy trailing plant. From Pakistan. Large flat flowers (4 cm). Brilliant mauve with white eye. Short-lived in the United Kingdom.

G. transbaicalicum This species, which is from Siberia, will perhaps in the future be considered a subspecies of *G. pratense* instead of an independent species, writes Yeo. Two varieties of the species: a low (25 cm) variety with dark bluish purple flowers and another taller variety that greatly resembles *G. pratense*.

G. trilophum Annual from Africa, Asia and Iran. Small flowers (1 cm). Dark pink with dark veins.

G. wilfordii Closely related to *G. thunbergii*. Very small flowers.

G. yesoense 30–40 cm. From Japan. The leaves are indented in the same way as *G. sanguineum*. Pink with dark veins or white without veins. Requires a moist environment.

G. yunnanense From China (Yunnan) and northern Burma. Large flowers (3–4 cm). Pink with black stamens. The rare white variety is sometimes called *G. candicans*, which is generally held to be a synonym.

Address List

Nurseries

Australia

Nutshell Perennial Nursery and Plant Farm, Softhaven, Campbell Street, Newbridge, New South Wales 2795.
Tel. (+61) (02) 6368 1035;
e-mail: nutshellperennials@ix.net.au.

Michael Pitkin, Viburnum Gardens, 8 Sunnyridge Road, Arcadia, New South Wales 2159. Tel. (+61) (02) 9653 2259. Fax. (+61) (02) 9653 1840.

Woodbridge Nursery, P.O. Box 90, Woodbridge, Tasmania 7162.
Tel/Fax. (+61) (03) 6267 4437.
(www.woodbridgenursery.com.au)

Austria

Sarastro-Stauden, Ort 131, 4974 Ort/Innkreis. Tel. (+43) 7751 8424 Fax. (+43) 7751 8424–3
(www.sarastro-stauden.com)

Denmark

Caroline Mathildestiens Planteskole, Caroline Mathildesti 51, 2950 Vedbæk.
Tel. (+45) 4566 0332.
(www.mathildestien.dk)

Helenas Stauder, Tyrstingvej 31, 8740 Brædstrup. Tel. (+45) 7576 1661.
(www.helenas-stauder.dk)
During the production of this book, the Danish publishers had a partnership with Helenas Stauder, which considerably increased its range. The nursery offers a wide selection of the geraniums featured in the book.

Holland

Coen Jansen—Vaste Planten, Ankummer Es 13, 7722 RD Dalfsen
Tel. (+ 31) 529 434086;
Fax. (+31) 529 436889.

Kwekerij 'De Hessenhof', Hessenweg 41, 6718 TC Ede. Tel. (+31) 318 617334;
Fax. (+31) 318 612773. (www.hessenhof.nl)

Germany

Annemarie Eskuche, Staudenkulturen am Söhnholz, 29664 Ostenholz.
Tel.(+ 49) 5167 287.
(www.stauden-eskuche.de)

Gärtnerei Simon, Staudenweg 2, 97828 Marktheidenfeld. Tel. (+49) 9391 3516;
Fax. (+49) 9391 2183.
(www.gaertnerei-simon.de)

United Kingdom

Axletree Nursery, which is frequently mentioned in the book, was a nursery run by David Hibberd but, unfortunately, it no longer exists.

Beeches Nursery, Village Centre, Ashdon, Saffron Walden, Essex CB10 2HB.
Tel. (+44) 01799 584362;
Fax. (+44) 01799 584421.
(www.beechesnursery.co.uk)

Cranesbill Nursery, White Cottage, Stock Green, near Redditch, Worcestershire B96 6SZ. Tel. (+44) 01386 792414;
Fax. (+44) 01386 792280.
(www.cranesbillnursery.com)

Croftway Nursery, Yapton Road, Barnham, Bognor Regis, West Sussex PO22 0BH.
Tel. (+44) 01243 552121;
Fax. (+44) 01243 552125.
(www.croftway.co.uk)

Crûg Farm Plants, Griffiths Crossing, near Caernarvon, Gwynned, Wales LL55 1TU.
Tel./Fax. (+44) 01248 670232.
(www.crug-farm.co.uk)

Stillingfleet Lodge Nurseries, Stillingfleet, North Yorkshire YO19 6HP
Tel./Fax.(+44) 01904 728506.
(www.stillingfleetlodgenurseries.co.uk)

The Plantsman's Preference, Lynwood, Hopton Road, Garboldisham, Diss, Norfolk IP22 2QN.
Tel. (+44) 01953 681439.
(www.plantpref.co.uk)

United States of America

Geraniaceae, 122 Hillcrest Avenue, Kentfield, CA 94904.
Tel. (+1) (415) 461–4168.
Fax. (+1) (415) 461–7209.
(www.geraniaceae.com)

Heronswood Nursery Ltd., 7531 NE 288th Street, Kingston, WA 98346. Tel. (+1) (360) 297–4172. Fax. (+1) (360) 297–8321
(www.heronswood.com)

Societies and publications

Denmark

Det Danske Haveselskab (The Danish Horticultural Society), Det danske Haveselskabs medlemsadministration (membership administration), Jægersborgvej 47, 2800 Lyngby.
Tel. (+45) 4593 6000. (www.haveselskab.dk)
Haven (magazine), Claecesholmvej 316, 8370 Hadsten. Tel. (+45) 8649 1734.

Germany

Gartenpraxis (magazine), Verlag Eugen Ulmer, Wollgrasweg 41, 70599 Stuttgart.
(www.gartenpraxis.de)

Sweden

The following offers a seed distribution service.
Trädgårdsamatörerna (Amateur gardeners) Anneli Juujärvi, Bäsna 272C, 781 95 Borlänge.
(www.tradgardsamatorerna.nu)

United Kingdom

The following also offer a seed distribution service.
The Alpine Garden Society (AGS) AGS Centre, Avon Bank, Pershore, Worcestershire WR10 3JP.
(www.alpinegardensociety.org)

Geraniaceae Group
Peter Starling, 22 Northfield, Girton, Cambridge CB3 0OG.
(The Register of Geranium cultivar names for which the society is responsible can be viewed at www.hardygeraniums.com)

Hardy Plant Society (HPS)
This society has a special interest group, the Hardy Geranium Group, for members who are particularly interested in cranesbills. The Hardy Plant Society, Little Orchard, Great Comberton, near Pershore, Worcestershire WR10 3DP.
(www.hardy-plant.org.uk)

Royal Horticultural Society
80 Vincent Square, London, SW1P 2PE.
(www.rhs.org.uk)

Above: *Geranium* ×*oxonianum* (probably 'Rødbylund') used as ground cover.

Bibliography

Bath, T. & J. Jones. 1994. *The Gardener's Guide to Growing Hardy Geraniums.* England: David & Charles.

Brackenbury, J. 1995. *Insects and Flowers. A Biological Partnership.* England: Blandford.

Clifton, R. T. F. 1995. *Geranium Family Species Check List.* Part 2 *Geranium.* The Geraniaceae Group.

Hardy Geraniums for the Garden. 2001. England: The Hardy Plant Society, 2001.

Hibberd, D. 2003. *Hardy Geraniums.* RHS Wisley Handbook. London, England: Cassell.

Hinkley, D. J. 1999. *The Explorer's Garden.* Portland, Oregon: Timber Press.

Jansen, C. 1997. *Geranium für den Garten.* Germany: Ulmer.

RHS Plant Finder 2003–2004. London, England: Dorling Kindersley.

Victor, D. X. *The Register of Geranium Cultivar Names.* England: The Geraniaceae Group. (www.hardygeraniums.com)

Yeo, P. F. 2001. *Hardy Geraniums.* New Edition, London, England: B. T. Batsford.

Online information

www.forlagetgeranium.dk. This Danish website contains up-to-date information on plant collectors with sales, plants, gardens to visit with numerous geraniums, plant markets where collectors will be present and other relevant information on geraniums.

Pictures of geraniums

www.crug-farm.co.uk
www.glendalegeraniums.co.uk
www.marksgardenplants.com
www.natuurlijk-eentuin.nl/geraniums/geraniums.html
www.overthegardengate.net/garden/archives/default.asp

Geranium forum

www.gardenweb.com

Other

www.geraniaceae.com/geraniums.html

G. 'Blue Sunrise'

Index